# A short history of the Netherlands

*second revised edition, 1973*

**Allert de Lange bv, Amsterdam**

# A short history of the Netherlands

**by Ivo Schöffer**

*William of Orange*

## Colophon

Cover-design, Hans Versteeg, Amsterdam
lay-out, Hans Versteeg, Amsterdam
maps, C.P.D., The Hague
illustrations, Rijksmuseum, Amsterdam; Koninklijk Instituut voor de Tropen, Amsterdam; A.N.P.-photo, Amsterdam; Joop Dorst, Gouda; Kees Molkenboer, Rotterdam; Bart Hofmeester, Rotterdam
printed by G. Kolff & Co., Amsterdam

ISBN 90 6133 076 9
© Allert de Lange bv, Amsterdam

# Contents

# Preface

A *short* history omits a great deal of or barely touches upon many matters which deserve more attention. The list of books at the end of this volume might be of some help to those who want to know more. On the other hand, the condensed character of this short history may make the introduction to a complicated subject clearer.

A short *history* cannot be limited to the political aspect only. Economic, social and cultural aspects also deserve attention. Despite the book's limited range it attempts to do just that.

A short history of the *Netherlands* takes as its starting-point the history of the territory of today as it is enclosed by the North Sea, Germany and Belgium. Looking back into the past, however, such boundaries become much vaguer.

At one time this territory was part of the Roman Empire, at another (during the greater part of the Middle Ages) one comes across quite separate feudal states like Holland, Gelre and Brabant, whose mutual ties were of rather external significance. For two periods in history, one during the 15th and extending into the 16th century, the other between 1815 and 1830, the Netherlands were linked up in some institutional way or other with the country known today as Belgium. Without, however, neglecting such facts in the past, the emphasis of this book will be on what is called 'the Netherlands' today.

Another choice of emphasis and direction had to be made. For obvious reasons more attention is paid to modern history than to the past. A glimpse at the contents will show this emphasis convincingly.

The use of some terms has, finally, to be explained. When writing about 'the Low Countries', the author has 'the Netherlands' together with Belgium in his mind. When 'the Netherlands' are mentioned without further explanation the contemporary kingdom is meant. Some inevitable irritation might be caused by the use of this same term when the author includes the Dutch-speaking areas in Belgium (and even a smaller part of north-western France) in a rather more linguistic-cultural sense.

But this complicating use of the same term will always be explicitly indicated.

For most foreigners, however, the use of the name 'Holland' has to be explained. For many reasons 'Holland' has often been synonymous for 'Netherlands'. Dutch people living in Overijssel or Groningen will say, however, that they go 'to Holland' when they visit the west of their country. 'Holland' will thus be used consistently for the western part of the Netherlands only. In the past, this (smaller) Holland had been first a separate feudal 'county' (graafschap) during the greater part of the Middle Ages to become, after the Dutch Revolt, during the 17th and 18th centuries, a semi-autonomous province within the federated Republic of the Seven Provinces. It is only after 1795 that this Holland became part of a centralized state, without losing its regional name of Holland or its institutional status as the provinces of North- and South-Holland within a Kingdom of eleven provinces.

This terminological preamble indicates in itself how complicated a history of the Netherlands really is. Let us hope that this small book will be of some help to disentangle the complicated development of what we call 'the Netherlands' today.

# 1     The oldest inhabitants

Nature films showing the development of some natural phenomenon in an accelerated sequence by using photographs taken over a long period, are well known and often shown. A plant springs from the soil, the bud swells, the flower bursts open and wilts again, all within one minute. The camera is set to take pictures at regular intervals in order to show rapidly what happened. In the writing of history the same procedure is used, with the one difference that the historian does not select one photograph a day, or a week, but perhaps one a year or a century. He cannot do otherwise because he depends on what the past has left to him for use. Archeologists are in an even worse position: they juggle with hundreds and even thousands of years.

Let us try to make our 'natural life' film one showing the development of that tiny corner of the globe where today the Low Countries are found. Pictures taken at intervals of, say, a thousand years will be shown and progress speeded up enormously. The first picture shows these Low Countries as part of the sea - a deep bay as it were in the coastline of the North Sea. Then - some 250,000 years ago -

new land was formed through deposition of mud by the large rivers we now call the Rhine and the Meuse, which flowed into this bay, cutting deep furrows. At a period about 200,000 years ago temperatures started to fall and the greater part of this muddy new land was gradually covered by a huge icecap. Some 80,000 years later the temperature rose gradually and the icecap started to melt very slowly. As a result an extensive plain was exposed, reaching far beyond the present coastline and sloping down towards the sea. With the melting of the icecap the sea started to rise and about 5500 BC a large part of this wide land was flooded again. Another five hundred years later the rising sea-level and strong storms forced a passage between those areas of land which we today call England and France, and the Straits of Dover were born. Masses of sand were washed ashore by the tides along the already flooded land to the north of these straits, and a broad line of dunes was built up in a south-north direction which could protect the hinterland and the flooded areas against further marauding by the sea. Only the mouths of the big rivers made gaps in this row of dunes, and behind this protective wall of sand there gradually formed deltas and islets, and a rich vegetation developed in stagnant waters and swamps, bordered by the edges of sand and clay which were deposited by the rivers along their banks. In the swamps peat bog was formed which later became dry land. But the sea relentlessly gnawed away at her own work - the dunes - and from the Middle Ages onwards in particular great gaps appeared in the weakest stretches along this line of defence, usually near the widening of the river mouths. Thus was formed in the south of the Netherlands the group of islands known today as Zeeland. In the north, the Waddenzee became an inner water with many outlets to the North Sea along the 'wadden'-isles. Finally that large inland sea, the Zuyder Zee, also started to expand, which until recent times helped to give this country its peculiar shape.

With the same incredible speed we shall have to flit through the few pictures available to illustrate the history of human life in this area. Some accidental discoveries in the soil bear testimony to what must have happened through these hundreds of centuries: for archeologists these data

10

serve as vaulting poles for jumping through time. As may be expected, the first traces of human life were found in the eastern areas of the country. There the soil was and always has been dry, mostly sandy, and relatively hilly. In the Veluwe area (in the centre of the country just south of the old Zuyder Zee) stone objects have been found probably dating as far back as 200,000 to 180,000 years. They are clumsily cut to serve as axeblades or spear points. A human skull, found during excavations for a canal in Twente, east of the Veluwe area, can be dated about 30,000 BC. Other findings in the Veluwe area and in Friesland (in the north) prove the existence of human life in these areas 10,000 years later. This time the objects are of a more varied character: tools in fact, suggesting the mastery of more advanced techniques among these hunting and fishing tribes. Knives, scratchers, piercers and needles are cut from stone. The way of life of these tribes about 20,000 BC may have corresponded to that of the Eskimoes of today: the inhabitants of the Netherlands were then apparently hunting reindeer in the Dutch tundra.

But now at last we can slow down. More data become available, giving us a fuller understanding of what was going on in this country. Between 3000 and 2000 BC new tribes seem to have migrated into the country, possibly offshoots of a culturally larger and more coherent group of people presumably centred in the Baltic area. The same pottery, the same kind of graves have been found in both places. These newcomers to the Netherlands were not exclusively hunters or fishermen - they tilled the soil and herded cattle. Their way of life demanded a higher degree of sophistication, a more developed organization. They became real settlers and were successful, in harnessing nature and domesticating animals to a certain extent. They, however, felt themselves guided by higher divine powers and worshipped their dead. They mastered the techniques not only of sharpening and polishing stone, but also of making pottery. Most impressive are the boulder graves found in Drente, in the north-east of the country, the so-called 'Hunebeds', of which the larger ones, near Borger and Havelte, were communal graves. The burial trench is bordered lengthwise by large upright boulders which are covered by long slabs. Probably the bodies of the dead were piled up in this stone shelter and then covered with sand and earth. How could the builders have moved these masses of rock to put them in position? Probably with the aid of tree trunks serving as rollers and levers, and artificial sand hills, against which the boulders were rolled: these hills would then be dug away and the boulders would topple over. These boulder graves may be less impressive than gigantic constructions like Stonehenge in Wiltshire (England), but they do show that the hunebed builders were deeply attached to the burial rites of their dead and were certainly highly adept in the building of such tombs. The quantities of pottery found in many of these tombs prove that neighbours regularly brought food to the dead. This pottery is well shaped and decorated and must have found its way beyond the original territory of the hunebed builders. Similar beakers and urns have been found in the Veluwe area.

The so-called 'beaker'-tribes are of later date (maybe some centruries later). Several relics of their existence have been left in the Veluwe area in particular. The pottery has its special shape and decoration: one finds bellshaped beakers, decorated urns with rope motifs, etc. The layman's attention will once again be drawn to the burial grounds - burial mounds this time. The dead were buried individually, laid in a space surrounded by vertical logs, and covered by sand and pebbles. Here too it was customary to donate gifts to the dead, and on this account the mounds still yield rich collections of interesting objects today. It is thought that these beaker tribes settled in this country for a long period, spreading their settlements in the course of time over a large area. Burial mounds have been found as far apart as Drente, in the north-east, and North Brabant, south of the big rivers. Through the different layers of buried relics of these tribes one can trace the gradual development from one generation to the next. The fact that bronze objects have been found, though in small quantities, proves that there were contacts between these beaker tribes and other tribes in central Europe.

Not until the 7th century BC do marked changes become apparent. New elements in the population, new ways of life, appear in the Low Countries. Celtic and Germanic tribes apparently entered the country, probably in small groups over a long period of time, mixing gradually with the people already settled here. Relations with Gallia (the France of today) and the Rhine regions (western Germany) can be traced in the southern and central areas of the Netherlands; influences from the Baltic and north German regions are in evidence in the east (Twente and Drente). Burial mounds made way for the so-called urn-fields. The dead were cremated now, their ashes put in urns and then in a systematic manner interred in one special field. Dwellings and utensils, as compared with those of the beaker tribes, changed in shape and appearance to such an extent as to suggest in some areas incidences of invasion and alien domination instead of gradual immigration.

With these Germanic and Celtic tribes settling on Dutch soil we leave prehistory behind us and enter the age of history proper. For the first time we can learn something about the life of these inhabitants from written sources: the Romans handed down their information to us in this way.

*'Hunebed'*

*7th century BC - 4th century AD*

At the time when the Romans entered the territory - about the beginning of our era - the Low Countries were an out-of-the-way corner of Europe. The tribes settled here, spread thinly over a large area, were an offshoot of more densely populated settlements in Gallia an Germania. The country itself had not much to offer. Swampy plains stretched out for miles behind the dunes, interspersed with stretches of turf and moors. The rising sea-level threatened the broad defences during storms, while at high tide the sea swept away large parts of the land. Only the higher areas and the fertile clay along the riverbanks were safe places for settlers to dwell. The Frisians, a Germanic tribe which had entered from northern Germany around 300 BC, settled in the north-east, the Groningen and Friesland of today. In the flat plains, to escape the strong and frequent floods of the sea, the Frisians were compelled to raise earthen platforms on which they built their dwellings. Thus the Frisian 'terps' originated: piled up mounds in a flat, low land. Rich territory for archeologists these terps are - they can be exposed layer by layer and offer an abundance of clues showing chronologically in each layer the different living arrangements. At least 900 terps must have been artificially built up by human hands in this northern part of the Netherlands. The Roman author Pliny did not think very highly of the Frisians, living on their hills and in their hovels. He describes them as 'seafarers whenever the surrounding areas are flooded by the sea, but shipwrecked as soon as the waters recede, chasing the fish that tries to escape with the current'. In reality, living conditions were more favourable than Pliny thought and the level of civilization certainly higher. Decorated pottery has been found in the lowest and therefore oldest layers of the terp. Wrought bronze ornaments and pins, woven mats and farming implements bear witness to techniques far from primitive. Those Frisians must have been quite well dressed for the period. Many of them had large stables with cattle, they tilled the land with hoes and spades, they grew flax and perhaps barley, they probably mastered the art of weaving and their existence must have been further brightened by the hunting of big game. Antlers of deer and elk, often worked into tools, teeth of wild boar and bear, have been found in the mounds: even the aurochs must have lived in these parts.

Far less is known of the other Germanic tribes which lived in other areas of the Low Countries: the Caninefats in the dunes bordering the Dutch coast, and the so-called Batavians in the Waal and Rhine basins. South of the great rivers lived some Celtic-speaking tribes of which the Nervii and the Ubii occupied some regions of the extreme south. It would be incorrect to picture these people as living very primitively, as earlier historians have said, although it is just as exaggerated to think of these Teutons and Celts as bearers of the highest possible civilization. Such exaggerations are perhaps partly due to Roman authors. Tacitus, for instance, wanted to hold up an image of a healthy, strong nation to his own degenerate, weak Roman world in 98 AD and wrote an idealized description of the Teutons. Pliny, on the other hand (62-113 AD), only saw the primitive and uncivilized aspects of the Germanic tribes. As is often the case, the truth lies in between. Compared to the Romans the Teutons were indeed primitive: they lived close to the soil. Town life was unknown to them. But in their own field they did reach a certain degree of organization, technical skill and civilization. Class differences, for example, did already exist - there were gentry and free men and slaves captured in warfare. Family ties were very close and embraced a larger clan than just the small family of father, mother and children. Such ties were indeed so important that if one member of the clan were attacked the other members would come to his defence (blood vengeance) and only the payment of rigidly specified blood-fees could prevent vengeance. In general, the Germanic tribes favoured monogamy and women had an important task in the household. They did the weaving, worked in the fields, had the care of the family, and they certainly had their say - although the family organization as such was patriarchal. All Teuton and Celtic tribes in the Netherlands can be said to have been fairly civilized and in spite of their frequently close contact with the Romans they preserved a great deal of their own traditions and organizations, not always to their disadvantage.

To the Romans, the Netherlands were nothing more than an out-of-the-way corner of their empire. When Caesar conquered the more densely populated Gallia, his legions invaded the Dutch territory along the banks of the Rhine. The area south of the Rhine could be considered to have belonged to the Roman empire from 57 BC, and was thoroughly romanized. But, although the Romans did penetrate north of the Rhine, this did not result in a definite submission of the Frisians or other tribes in that region. The Rhine in fact remained the natural defence-line for the Romans, and as a result Roman influence was regionally highly varied. The extreme south, the present South Limburg, was strongly romanized. Mosa Trajectum (Maastricht) was founded at the junction of several Roman roads, connecting the Roman legions with the provinces of Belgica (the Low Countries south of the Rhine) and with such centres of defence as Cologne, Rheims and Trier. These roads attracted tradesmen, facilitated the building of large Roman-type farms (villas), and the foundation of small industrial settlements wherever raw material was available. Maastricht and its surroundings benefited from this trade and industry, and even today one can find typical Roman farms in South Limburg: living quarters and stables built around a rectangular courtyard, with one gate.

The actual Roman front (limes) stretched along the Rhine in the north, and Teuton attacks had to be repeatedly repulsed. Two major rebellions were really dangerous for the Romans, because in both, troops allied to the Romans defected and sided with the rebels: one in the year 9 AD, led by a man named Arminius, and one in 67 AD when Batavian auxiliary troops of the Romans mutinied under the leadership of Claudius Civilis. Along the banks of the Rhine the Romans literally dug themselves in: a sort of no man's land was created north of the Rhine and no settling was allowed there. A solid highroad skirted the river, dotted with relay stations for horses, strongholds and army camps (castra and castella). Camps of this type were at Noviomagus (Nijmegen), Fectio (Vechten), Trajectum (Utrecht) and Valkenburg (near Leiden). One small stretch of this Roman road still exists in the neighbourhood of Wageningen. The furthermost fortress of Brittenburg, beyond Katwijk, is now submerged under the sea. The Romans must have considered this defence-line a source of constant danger: troops were permanently kept in the camps and the roads between them were continually patrolled. Recent excavations at Valkenburg have shown that the Romans built very strong fortresses there.

In the far north, the Frisians were never subjugated by the Romans and probably kept the Roman legions permanently from their soil. But many objects of Roman origin found in the terps prove close contact with the Romans and cannot exclude at least a definite Roman influence. Roman soldiers, after all, were followed by Roman merchants, and these travelling people brought with them not only Roman products but Roman techniques, Roman beliefs and Roman knowledge. The army camps were soon surrounded by small trade settlements: near Nijmegen there is evidence of one with about 3,000 inhabitants. Roads developed traffic and trade. Shipping routes down the Rhine and the Vecht, across the still small Almere (later Zuyder Zee, now IJsselmeer), carried Roman influence beyond the borders of the actual Roman occupation. In order to eliminate a dangerous sea voyage, a canal (the canal of Corbulo) was dug from the Meuse outlet to the mouth of the Rhine (at that time near Katwijk). Fectio was the most northern port of Roman power and served as an important transit station for shipping to Roman-occupied Britain. Through these contacts with the Romans, Teutons learned the use of the potter's wheel, accepted and used Roman coins, copied style motifs in their ceramics, and borrowed thoughts and ideas from Roman religion. Thanks to this Roman influence Christianity also penetrated the area in South Limburg for a short while during the 4th century but ended again shortly afterwards. At a much later date the new organization of the Christian faith also followed Roman traditions and the Roman organizational way of government. The old Roman provinces became archbishoprics, civitates bishoprics, Rheims and Cologne the ecclesiastical centres. And for a greater part of the Middle Ages the Roman highroads were to remain the most important routes for traffic, whilst the old Roman settlements at many crossroads were to develop into flourishing cities.

Not until 200 AD did the Roman defence line in the Netherlands begin to crumble, as elsewhere, and as the Netherlands were the most far-flung post for the Romans, they were the first to be evacuated. Together with the Romans the Batavian tribes disappeared from history, having probably moved south with their Roman allies. Complete evacuation, though, was very slow and in the south it did not happen until the 4th century. There were no real battles in this area, but the Roman retreat coincided with the immigration of Saxons and Angles in the north, Franks in the south. And these 'invasions' brought new problems not just for the people of that time but also for the historians of today.

# 3    Frisians and Franks

*4th - 10th century*

After the retreat of the Romans, written records of the history of the Low Countries vanished for a long time - a sad loss to the historian, particularly for a period of great change about which we would like to know so much. During the migrations of the third and fourth centuries the actual foundations were laid for the future development of the Netherlands. From the earliest post-Roman records it appears that the population in this area settled down, but we are left wondering whether whole tribes swept into the east of the country, or only small bands of better-armed individuals. What had happened to the settled tribes: were they displaced or absorbed by the newcomers? In the south, the influx of Germanic tribes certainly meant the disappearance of romanized civilization together with the language barrier which was probably pushed far south of the area that formed the Roman/Germanic language frontier in the Middle Ages.

It is not certain to what extent the settled Teutonic tribes played a part in this development as opposed to the influence of the newcomers. As early as the 8th century this Teutonic language group, spreading far into the Germany of today, was referred to as 'theodisk'. From this 'theodisk' two separate languages were to develop over the centuries: one that would be spoken in the Netherlands (cf. 'theodisk' with 'Diets' from which the word 'Dutch' is derived), and German, used in the many regions east of the Low Countries (called 'Duits' in the Netherlands, 'Deutsch' in Germany). It was not until the 13th century that Dutch became a written language.

On the whole it seems that the newly arrived tribes, Angles and Saxons north of the rivers, Franks along the river banks, reinforced rather than displaced the tribes already occupying the area. Some of these new groups passed through and migrated to other territories: Angles and Saxons crossed the sea to England, many Franks moved on to Gallia, others stayed behind. Possibly some of the older inhabitants were swept along with the current. For the Frisian tribes this influx and movement of peoples had its importance because they were probably more influenced by new Germanic groups, intermixing with them and influencing their habits and language, than ancient Frisian historians cared to admit. The nationalist historian preferred to see the 'free Frisians' as an autochtonous, independent nation with its own separate and great past. But excavations of the terps prove that the arrival of the Angles was for the Frisians of great importance, and it may be assumed that many Angles and Saxons became Frisians themselves. It is far less certain whether Saxons settled in really significant numbers in the present provinces of Drente and Overijssel. Recent research seems to indicate that in this case the influx of the Franks was more important than any Saxon settlement. As for the southern areas, it is fairly certain that many Franks colonized this territory - perhaps all the way down to the river outlets.

Lasting consequences of these new settlements do not become apparent until many centuries later: not until the 7th and 8th centuries did Frisian and Frankish expansion pinpoint their significance. Too little is known of these developments, but they can be more or less imagined. Although some land was reclaimed along the IJssel, the actual population remained scant and dispersed. The rising waters, the marshy soil of many places in the west, the still extensive forests and woods in the east, undoubtedly retarded development. Agriculture (rye), cattle-breeding (sheep and cattle) and fishing continued to be the main means of existence. Up till about 1000 AD there is little likelihood that there was any large-scale building of dykes: the raising of terps continued in the areas most affected by the rising sea-level. But it is quite possible that Frisian shipping and trade began to develop early in this period. Since the time of the Romans, coined money had remained in circulation, including gold coins captured during earlier sorties into the dwindling Roman realm, but it was not until the 7th century that Frisian trade reached any importance. From that time onwards Frisians as traders and shippers spread far into Europe. Due to their geographical position and some familiarity with the sea, the Frisians had become able navigators and possibly their rather poor terp-like existence at home drove them on to try their luck elsewhere. From the 7th century Frisian expansion became quite impressive: trade settlements were found in York (Great Britain), Birka (Sweden), Schleswig (Denmark) and in particular along the Rhine in Cologne, Mainz and Trier. 'Frisian' cloth, probably of English and Flemish origin, was the main commodity, other trading products ranging from amber, timber and grain from the north, tin, lead and wool from England, to iron tools from the Low Countries. The actual centre of the Frisian trade expansion had developed on the banks of the Rhine in Dorestad (near the present Wijk bij Duurstede), a Frankish-Frisian settlement near the main rivers, not too far from the sea, but also not too exposed to attacks by pirates. The political consequences of this Frisian trade expansion were unimportant: only for a short period during the reign of 'King' Radbod (679 - 719) does any real Frisian political power seem to have reached the main rivers of the area. The growing power of the Franks soon pushed the Frisians back to their territory, which today comprises the provinces of Friesland and Groningen, and the West Friesland area in the province of North Holland, and finally even subjected them.

The political expansion of the Franks had therefore a more lasting influence on the development of the Netherlands, both socially and culturally, than the Frisian expansion ever had, and this in spite of the fact that the actual centre of power of the Franks was situated outside the Dutch lands in the north of France. In ancient Gallia Frankish power had been firmly entrenched by the chieftain Clovis (480 - 511) and the King's minister Charles Martel (714 - 741). It was not until the reign of a descendant of Martel that Frankish power extended northwards; linked to this impressive conquest is the name of this descendant: Charlemagne (768 - 814). During Roman supremacy the Low Countries and particularly the northern parts had been a far-away corner of the empire, but this country in the north was much nearer to the headquarters of the Franks. Charlemagne's favourite residences were the palatinates (fortified centres of large agricultural demenses) at Aix-la-Chapelle (Aachen), Trier and Nijmegen. Thus this ingenious Frankish royal system embraced parts of the Netherlands, and Frankish influence radiated widely from this circle of royal residences over the outer lands. Agricultural innovations of an organizational kind carried through during the period of Frankish power had important consequences in the northern area also. The three-yearly crop-rotation system, by which one alternating third of the land had to lie fallow, ensuring both sedentariness for the farmers and regular crops, was of Frankish origin and was gradually applied in the Low Countries. The governmental system of Charlemagne which, out of pure necessity rather than calculation, delegated secular power to local rulers and lords, formed the basis of the feudal system that prevailed over most of the Netherlands during the Middle Ages.

Finally, Frankish power was the force behind the introduction of Christianity. In the south, in ancient Gallia, Christianity had succesfully ousted other beliefs in the 7th century, but in the north it was succesful only in the course of the 8th century with the help of the Frankish conquest and Frankish arms. It is true that the actual mission in the Netherlands was started mostly by Irish and Anglo-Saxon missionaries and reinforced by zealous preachers from the German church provinces. But perhaps the Franks supported this foreign initiative; they most certainly gave substantial help by the threat of arms.

Willibrord the Anglo-Saxon started his mission among the Frisians in 690 and chose Trajectum, the old Roman settlement (Trecht, Utrecht), for the seat of this Frisian church province. Only after the Frisians had been finally conquered by the Franks (in 734, on the banks of the Boorne) did the entire area as far as the Lauwers Sea lie open to the mission. The introduction and sometimes wilful imposing of a new religion, entirely strange to the tribes, must have seemed part of the Frankish lust for conquest and submission. Resistance against christianization was very fierce indeed, and a poignant token of this resistance was the murder of Bonifacius by the Frisians in 754, at the time when this great missionary was already honoured in Germany as a saint. Liudger had to undertake the final conversion of the Frisians from Münster between 780 and 792. Conversion, however, was often not spontaneous and compulsory mass baptism, imposed on conquered tribes by the Franks, occurred several times. As a consequence conversion was sometimes no more than an outward appearance and it was several generations before the real Christian Church could function in a more satisfactory way: under the veneer of the new religion the old heathen beliefs frequently showed through. In this respect the new Church was pliant enough: many Teuton pagan festive days were preserved, though explained by Christian symbolism. The ancient Teuton Yule, honouring the renewed lengthening of the days, was changed into Christmas, honouring the birth of the Light of Christ. Pagan traditions continued to exist side by side with Christian ones: Easter eggs, ancient symbols of fertility and spring, now lent a decorative touch to the new Christian feast of the Resurrection. Crude forms of what we call superstition, such as witch persecution and exorcism, were sanctioned and supported by the Church in the Middle Ages. For many pagan Teutons the decisive factor in conversion was whether the God of the Christians proved to be mightier than their own gods. The preacher who could spend the night in a holy forest unharmed, the missionary who would smash the powerful idol without the wrath of the gods annihilating him, was far more convincing than any amount of pious preaching and praying. Real penetration of Christianity into their minds and hearts would take decades or even centuries. But during the 8th and 9th centuries the foundations were laid, politically and socially, as well as in matters of church and religion, for the Christian Middle Ages.

# 4     Political disintegration

*9th - 14th century*

Frankish domination in the Netherlands lasted no more than a century: long enough to deeply influence the future development of the country, but too short to shape a unanimous well-organized nation. For a proper understanding of the inevitable disintegration that followed, it should be remembered that during the Frankish period old tribal relationships and organizations had continued to exist. In fact, even during the seemingly strong and conquering reign of Charlemagne, tensions developed in the empire and as soon as death removed the strong hand of the great organizer and conqueror, the entire realm fell apart. The plunderings and conquests of the Scandinavian pirates, Norsemen and Danes - however drastic their invasions were for the coast dwellers of the Netherlands in particular - were attendant incidents rather than a true cause of disintegration. Agriculture was the main means of subsistence, more so than during Roman times. Trade, although it had never entirely disappeared, has lost its importance, and especially in the areas farther away from the old Roman trade-routes, the great rivers and the highroads, there was a tendency to fall back upon exchange of products, thus eliminating the use of money. The system of government introduced by the Franks had, moreover, encouraged such tendencies, since the central authority, unable to keep the realm under complete central control - traffic, after all, was primitive and slow - had to delegate power. Great landlords, 'counts' (graaf) sometimes also office-bearers of the Church, were charged with authority over specified districts (gouwen), usually the areas where they resided. As the strength of the central power slackened, the power of these vassal counts increased. In the Netherlands, in particular, only too accessible to the invading Norsemen from the sea and cut off from land traffic by the many swamps and wide rivers, this growth in the power of the local aristocracy was inevitable.

Within the smaller districts, social relations also tended towards a greater dependence of the people upon their lords. Many free farmers felt compelled - because of the uncertain times and under pressure - to cede the rights to their own small plots of land in exchange for legal and military protection from their lords and the guarantee of a part of the yield of their plots. These former free men belonged from then onwards to the landed property, the domain of a lord. They became serfs, not real slaves, dependent on the aristocracy but with specified rights for themselves. They could not be bought or sold and in exchange for certain services and products from their lands they 'belonged' to the land with their families. Curiously enough, at least in the Netherlands, real slavery disappeared during and after the Frankish period. The reason for this is still unknown. In Friesland, where in general people remained free and the feudal system had very little hold, and in Holland, the fight against the invading water strengthened the cause of individual liberty, and the young Christian Church, in its zeal for conversion, freed many converted slaves and generally encouraged the liberation of slaves.

In the meantime, a complicated network of mutual dependence and subordination had been created within the aristocratic circles of the greater landlords. Frankish power readily adapted itself to this development: the direct vassals of the crown were allowed to delegate power over smaller parts of their properties to others called subfiefs, and this system of mutual interdependence and different forms of subordination brought about the so-called feudal system. By the time the original purpose of temporary delegation of kingly power to his direct vassals was lost through the introduction of hereditary rights and powers for the holders of the fiefs, intermarriage and inheritance created an extremely complicated situation among an aristocracy which became a separate class with very firm and often almost autonomous power on a local level. Events which coincided with and contributed to this disintegration are perhaps a more striking illustration of what happened. There were the disastrous invasions of Norsemen, mostly Danes. These swift navigators could land at the most vital centres of the country and disappear again with rich loot before any countermeasures could be taken. The Frisian trade settlements along the sea shore suffered most. Even the trade and shipping centre of Dorestad had to endure a succession of plunderings and ravages, from which it did not recover (834 - 850), and Frisian trade in fact succumbed under these ceaseless assaults. Even the granting of typical feudal rights to some Danish chieftains had little effect. Frankish kings were forced to make this concession in order to save on local coastal defence, but these Danes were certainly not obedient vassals to the absentee king.

Another development of equal importance followed: the central power itself was weakened substantially. Disputes about the succession to the imperial throne after the death of Charlemagne caused constant new divisions and internal strife. For a period the Netherlands territory was formally ruled by an Emperor of Lorraine, and this powerless ruler was followed by Emperors of the so-called Holy Roman Empire of the Germans who tried as the highest feudal lords of all, in name at least, to wield this sceptre over the Netherlands. Formal and sometimes real intervention continued to be a factor in home affairs but it was more to the advantage of the local rulers on the spot than to the Emperor himself.

It is clear that all these developments and events gradually helped the local lords to get the best of it. They became hereditary authorities, owners of vast properties, in which many serfs worked for themselves but also for their masters. Only the local aristocracy, linked to them by many feudal rules, could be a nuisance. These local rulers also became patrons of monasteries and churches in their territories, judges and rulers at the same time. In this way one can find in the Netherlands a count of Holland, a descendant of one of these Danish chieftains, who extended his power over increasingly larger parts along the western seacoast. In Utrecht a bishop acquired worldly powers in the central (the Sticht bishopric) and eastern part of the country (called 'Oversticht': the later provinces of Overijssel and Drente). In between these territories of the bishop of Utrecht, a larger territory developed of which the local ruler was a count of Gelre, later duke of the same area that is today known as Gelderland. South of the rivers a powerful count of Flanders and later equally impressive dukes of Brabant and Limburg could be found. Only the Frisians in the North, in their area of origin, managed to keep the ruling feudal nobles away and with them the feudal system, by allowing rich farming lords to become untitled local aristocrats. These Frisians tried to protect themselves by means of a legendary royal right of full independence, supposedly granted to them by Charlemagne, but in fact nature came to their aid. The rising sea level had gradually turned the inland Flevolake (Almere) into an inland sea, the Zuyder Zee. The North Sea broke through the Wadden coast, creating a big gap between the Friso-Groningen and the West Frisian areas (north of Holland). Stubborn efforts by the counts of Holland to subjugate the Frisians across the water failed thanks to this natural obstacle. Only the West Frisians, cut off from their 'motherland' by the same natural obstacle, finally had to surrender.

It was not only the Frisians, however, who resisted attempts to subjugate them: in each district there were constant internal struggles among the minor vassals and sub-fiefs for or against their feudal ruler. They became, in the service of their count, bishop or duke, mounted well armed warriors, intensively trained in fighting on horseback, and they very soon became aware of their powers of intrigue at the cost of their masters. Many a large homestead belonging to this local aristocracy became a stronghold and eventually a citadel or castle. Then there were the dramatic rivalries between the counts, bishops and dukes themselves, with many shifts of power and territorial gains or losses. Before 1100 the 'Sticht' was by far the most important district north of the rivers. The election of its bishop was virtually the right of the Emperor of the Holy Roman Empire in Germany, and often the ruler enthroned at Utrecht received in this manner the formal support that helped to make him the pawn of German power politics in the west. The city of Utrecht, as the centre of the Church in the Netherlands and permanent seat of the bishop, was also a flourishing centre of traffic and trade. After 1100 the glory of Utrecht was to be overshadowed by that of Holland, whilst the influence of Gelre helped to undermine the right of election of bishops and the actual temporal power of this local ecclesiastical ruler.

Economically the position of the count of Holland was strong. Once he had succeedded in getting a firm hold on the outlets of the Rhine and Meuse he could levy tolls on the important river- and ocean-shipping trade. In 1018 he defeated an army of the Emperor of Lorraine, later on he captured West Friesland from the Frisians and Zeeland from the Flemish, and finally he gained influence in Utrecht. In the 13th century the counts of Holland ventured into major politics and carried out intrigues as minor partners to the Kings of England and France together with the count of Flanders and the duke of Brabant.

But the picture is not one of merely internal struggles. During the course of the 13th century the power of the more important lords within their own territories, such as Holland, Gelre or Brabant, had grown to such an extent that these lords, often against the wish of the local nobility, managed to unite under their rule the whole of their territory. They found the support they needed in the emerging cities. Judicial and governmental organizations developed, almost entirely controlled by these lords and their favourites. Real officialdom came into being only much later, but these organizations had their own special merits. Without them the country, in its separate territories, would have disintegrated through interior disputes into chaos, as, for example, happened in Friesland in the 14th and 15th centuries. The construction of the dyke system

and the foundation of the dyke boards in Holland would
have been impossible without the strong leadership of the
counts. Even in the cities - most of which owed their
development to the counts - the sovereign lords continued
to hold a certain degree of influence.

At the same time, things were certainly not easy for the
lordly power. In the 14th century Holland passed through a
terrible crisis in which the power of the count was at stake.
Disputes like those of the 'Hoeken' and 'Kabeljouwen' kept
Holland in a state of civil war for a long time; and in the
same way Gelre suffered from severe internal strife
between the clans and factions of the Heekerens and
Bronkhorsten. On the whole, however, the great lords
managed to get the better of these disputes, and
succeeded in saving their positions. When later on these
separate counties and dukedoms fell into the hands of one
ruler, a further unification of the governmental organization
was possible. The sovereign landlords had taken the lion's
share in preparing for such a union both politically and by
way of organizational tightening-up of power and
jurisdiction.

# The impact of the sea during the centuries

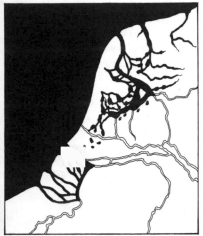

*during Roman times*

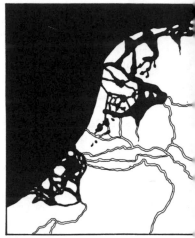

*9th century*

*13th century*

*17th century*

# 5      The struggle against the water

Geographical conditions and natural developments had a strong historical influence in the Netherlands. The country was in many ways a broad delta with large rivers spreading wide over flat and low lands. The coastal defences against the sea were partly strengthened by the high sand-dunes in the west, but were weakened on the other hand by the many outlets of these broad rivers which created numerous islands and large inner seas. Storms, high tides and the general rise of the sea-level created in the course of time ever greater problems. Undoubtedly large parts of the western coast would have been flooded completely by salt or sweet water at the end of the Middle Ages, had not human inventiveness and organization helped to save the soil by artificial means.

The rising sea-level was perhaps the greatest danger, in particular when high tides and storms caused sudden break-throughs. Living on terps was reasonably satisfactory as long as the floods were not too numerous or too widespread, and as long as the need for agricultural land was not as important as shipping and fishing: corn supplies came in from other areas by ship or cart. Floods, however, became more frequent and more severe, and the invasions of the Danes paralysed trade and cut off supplies of corn. The progressive brackishness of the soil, increasingly open to the waters behind the dunes via inner seas and widening rivers, became alarming. Probably as early as the 8th century large areas of the Maas (Meuse) and Waal were already protected by dams, perhaps even by dykes. But not until about 1000 did the inhabitants along the Zuyder Zee-coast of West Friesland start to build dykes systematically as a defence against the tide. Low dams were built up to connect one terp with the next, though later on dykes were constructed nearer the sea. Gradually new land, deposited by the sea outside the outer dykes, was walled in by new dykes, and in this way land defence could mean acquisition or at least reclamation of soil. Clay, grass mats, seaweed and logs formed the main building materials for the dykes. In comparison with the older dams, dykes were more systematically constructed with these materials and with sloping sides, in particular on the seaward side. Moreover, around 1200 a system of inner dykes along the rivers was developed, by which at high tides these rivers could be channelled to the sea-outlets. Sometimes a complete combination of such inner dyke-systems was built within a few decades to protect a vast area. During the reign of Count William I of Holland (1203 - 1222) the major part of South Holland, protected by dunes against the North Sea, was enclosed in a safe system of dykes to hold off tide-water coming from the sea into the rivers or high waters flowing down due to heavy rainfall or a rapid thaw in the Alps.

In the 13th century, this powerful dynasty of Dutch counts in Holland succeeded in building up an organization for the upkeep and inspection of the dykes which has served ever since as an example for all dyke and polder areas elsewhere (e.g. in Lower Germany, Slavic areas). It was the result of superior organizational talent and based upon improvisation and experience, and credit for this effort is due to William I. Organization was necessary to prevent each inhabitant from doing his own dyke-tending in his own small area of interest which resulted more often than not in neglect. Dyke-tending called for continuous care, not just in case of floods or break-throughs, because the water-logged soil and the condition of the dykes themselves caused a gradual sinking and sagging of the structure. Continuous care in a more systematic way could only be succesful by common effort, though on the other hand individual effort or initiative should never be relinquished. More than anything else this kind of defence against the water was a matter of a chain depending on its weakest link. Dyke bursts and inundations, which struck the country during the 12th and 13th centuries and were sometimes so terrifying that they were believed to be a second Flood, were grave warnings showing the need for an ever better organization. Each area protected by a system of dykes formed a polder district which was put in charge of an officer of the count: the so-called dyke-reeve, assisted by a board of local land-owning inhabitants: the polder board. At regular intervals three times a year the condition of the dykes was inspected. The board was given full advisory and in many ways discretionary and judicial power. It was the stated duty of each inhabitant of a polder district to tend to a certain part of the dyke and in times of stormy weather and rising tides all men were marshalled to guard the dykes and protect weak spots. There were times when, due to carelessness and lack of discipline, this sound organization did not work properly: floods were the penalties and reminders of such negligence. A heavy toll was paid during the dramatic floods of the 15th century, which caused unnecessary loss of land. But against this, common sense and a feeling of responsibility were able to tackle gigantic tasks: the preservation of the Zeeland isles, the reclaiming of the land where the Middelzee had struck a deep hole in the Frisian shore, the powerful Frisian dykes along that coast.

The constant battle with rain and surface water was not an easy one: there were in Holland, and in Friesland in particular, too many bogs and lakes behind the dykes and dunes, where only fishermen and huntsmen could make a living. The reclaiming of these swamps was also undertaken around the year 1000 and considerably speeded up during the reign of count Floris V of Holland (1256 - 1296). In the following centuries, land reclamation even developed into a special profession: shortage of arable land and lust for speculation stimulated such reclamation work. The increase in population and the need for better corn production made internal reclamation and colonization of such land necessary. Rich landowners must have foreseen that land-reclaiming would be a profitable business: they bought for that purpose acres of peat bog - often carefully divided into rectangular pieces - and got to work. Two parallel ditches were dug from one end to the other through the muddy area - the strip of land between the ditches was in this way piled up to serve as a road. Crossditches were then dug at rectangles to the first ones so that the water level would go down and fertile meadows and fields were thus drained and dried and could be leased or sold.

The drainage of fields, cut into rectangles by ditches, proved to be a constant problem which grew worse when the drained soil started to cave in. After all, these drained lands were low already and water tended to flow towards these lower areas. Drainage had to be organized therefore in a more permanent way. The first effort to get rid of the constant inflow of water with the aid of small mills driven by hand or horse power did not prove satisfactory, but human inventiveness found another solution. Around the year 1400 the first windmills were built in order to pump the water from the low-lying polder into the canals and rivers, often lying on a higher level. At first these mills were fixed to the ground and could only be used when a strong southwesterly wind, the most usual wind in the Netherlands, was blowing. Later, small mobile mills were built (known in Friesland as 'tjasker') which could be turned to catch every wind. In the course of time these mills proved to be too small and other larger ones were built, fixed to the ground, but with means of swivelling them on their base. These polders too were supervised by their own boards, run on more democratic lines than the sea-polder boards: they were formed by all the inhabitants of the polder (ingelanden). Large parts of Holland and Friesland have been reclaimed by this system of drainage and the use of windmills. Even peat bogs in England, Germany and Poland were drained by colonists coming from Holland. The reclaiming of land from the larger and deeper lakes took more capital and energy. There, extensive dykes had to be built first, then big pumping installations set up near these dykes and finally a more complicated draining system worked out. This often took years and productive results in the form of arable land would not show until much later. When during the 17th century Dutch traders and merchants acquired vast sums of money and started to look round for some investment, this type of polder reclamation was undertaken on a large scale, often with great losses for the first investors. The big lakes in West Friesland were drained in the 17th century and in later centuries even larger projects followed: the Haarlemmermeer (19th century) and the Zuyder Zee (20th century). But by this time tools and equipment had changed a good deal since the days of the spade, fork and wheelbarrow, when the first clods were thrown up to start a dyke.

# 6     Church and civilization

The structure of society in the Middle Ages seemed to be one of many small cells functioning independently. Politically, socially and economically the Netherlands appeared to be virtually disintegrated. One main artery, however, connected the many cells of the system, supplying so to say fresh blood to each cell, and bringing this blood from a wider connection which embraced the whole western Christian civilization. The unity of the Church within the Netherlands during the Middle Ages is evident, but on closer inspection each picture appears in its own light, with its own nuances, in time as well as space. For one thing, in the Netherlands the Church had a much more difficult job in fighting the remains of old pagan traditions of Teutonic origin than in the Latin countries. Although the history, at least of the Middle Ages and during the Middle Ages, is entirely recorded by the clergy, there must have been hosts of old stories handed down from generation to generation, which kept the Teutonic traditions alive in the minds of the people for a much longer period than the church authors in the pious revelations of their writings cared to admit. Sometimes, however, the smooth surface of official teachings and christian piety was rippled by tales about superstition, fear and agitation among the common people. The clergy branded these as inspirations of the devil in the shape of witchcraft, sorcery and heresy. But it seems fairer to think of them as the results of the worries of life, the poor environment, the fear of illness and death, often expressed in old pagan forms of ritual and exorcism. Equally difficult to overcome, no doubt, were the traditions of social organization which could not be incorporated into the wider and more orderly type of government of feudal society, or into the Church, with its different moral and ethical rules. Nevertheless clan organization and especially blood-feuds, old rules about marriage and family life continued to hold sway for a long time, beneath the official views of rulers and ecclesiastics. On the whole the Church was the main channel by which southern civilization penetrated and it was only gradually able to overcome the ancient pagan views and habits which were in many ways inferior to those of the Roman tradition. The final success of the Church was due to persuasion and gradualness rather than force and speed, though tension always remained in some form or other, among people, among groups, between the laity and the clergy. In every society, and certainly in the ones where conditions are relatively static, tensions are bound to rise and last. Yet the Church as such did not represent to the people an oppressive or subjugating force, particularly when the older generations who remembered the conversions by force had gone. To the laity, and most of all the simple farmer and villager, the Church became the centre of life outside their daily toil. Even their recreation, singing and music, story-telling and drama originated from the Church, and many, though perhaps not exceedingly pious or religiously minded, simply accepted the Church as the institution which clearly prescribed their duties and social conduct in order that by their way of life on this earth, they would be assured of peace and grace in the life hereafter. The Church did indeed offer this feeling of security and certainty, while also satisfying the needs of entertainment and creativity latent in every civilization. This explains why comparatively humbly-living people were prepared to make such huge sacrifices in order to build gigantic churches and cathedrals of unsurpassed beauty and magnificence, often much too large for the small communities who used the buildings for religious purposes. The wealthy donated entire properties, and later gold, jewels and precious stones, to churches and monasteries. The poor saved to make gifts of a few pennies or to light candles. The ties which bound the people to the Church were strong: all the main events in their lives - birth, adolescence, marriage and death - were linked to the Church by the sacraments and ceremonies. In particular the innate fear of sickness and death drove them to the Church; they were obvious daily dangers for everybody, with little remedy besides prayer and confession. Life was short; illness was mysterious and could be terrible, death came early for most. Wise and pious advisers, priests and confessors were there to offer guidance, whilst the monks and the nuns dedicated their lives to God in order to save souls.

There was a sharp division between the clergy and the laity. The clergy stood apart by their way of life, their work, their dress, and the rules according to which they had to live. Their vows of celibacy separated them from the laity because they had no family to look after - although many did not abide by these vows. The clergy was also distinguished by the fact that at least many of them could read and write and were thus able to know things which the laity neither could nor were supposed to know. Furthermore, life in the monasteries could be rather isolated, and this created an atmosphere of security and religious purpose different from the life of the laity. Many monasteries were strongholds of learning: an important heritage of Roman and Latin civilization, interwoven with the new Christian traditions, was preserved here and handed down. The use of Latin as the international church language kept the channels of communication with the rest of the Christian world wide open. It is possible that things were preserved, copied and repeated, rather than that new thoughts, stimulated by the old, were born, but nonetheless the choise of what should be preserved caused changes in emphasis, and most certainly a deal of what was left of the old classical tradition and knowledge was stored in these centres of civilization. The collections of manuscripts and books, chronicles and works of theology or philosophy were carefully kept in the libraries of these monasteries; generation after generation, by caring for these works and copying them, helped to preserve and to use what great civilizations had left behind.

Not only was the clergy clearly different from the laity, but internally the organization allowed a wide variety of activities and rules which created of course its own tensions and problems. In the wider church policy the dramatic rivalry for power between Emperor and Pope in the 11th and 12th centuries found its relatively small repercussions in the disputes between the Bishop of Utrecht and the Count of Holland. Not all clergymen took sides with the Bishop of Utrecht, who gradually lost his case against the growing power of the Count. There were tensions also between higher and lower clergy, between various religious orders. Who in fact could be strong enough to bear the superhuman task of spritiual leadership, exemplary conduct and complete annihilation of self? It is not surprising that carpenters chiselled the image of a fat priest lending an eager ear to the whisperings of the devil, tucked away under a magnificent pew or in a corner of a doorpost. It would be a mistake to expect every monastery to be a centre of science and culture: nor should it be forgotten that many women's convents founded in the Netherlands were more often than not a realistic solution to the dramatic problem caused by the surplus of women rather than the fulfilment of the spiritual and religious needs of the people.

And yet this Church, with all its weakness and failures, bore fruits of culture which in the Netherlands are still regarded as highlights in art and science. The church buildings are the most striking architectural features still preserved: the massive, towering buildings, symbols of safety and faith, are to this day outstanding landmarks. Two beautiful churches, in the so-called Roman style, were built in Maastricht in the 12th century; the Minster church of Roermond of one century later belonged to this kind of gigantic building. From France the Gothic style, soaring and graceful, characterized by pointed arches in buttresses, vaults and windows, was introduced, but like the Roman style it penetrated rather late into the Netherlands and never developed in the lavish and over-luxurious way it did elsewhere. It seemed as if Dutch soberness and matter-of-factness simplified its main features and held the style within the limits of this simplicity and directness. Utrecht Cathedral was started in the 14th century - an enterprise which in the end took three centuries to finish, with at times only a few able artisans continuing the construction. Perhaps also due to the nature of the building material the airy grace of the French gothic style has never quite been realized, but the red brick used gave Dutch cathedrals and churches their own characteristics. The St. Bavo at Haarlem illustrates this. Only the grand St. John's Cathedral at 's-Hertogenbosch is an almost perfect embodiment of heavenwards-soaring serenity.

Applied arts developed along with church and ecclesiastical building, and were used or at any rate often only preserved in the service of the churches. Only a combination of endless patience, great technical skill and a fine artistic feeling could yield the magnificent results shown by these crafts. Church treasures, church sculpture, carvings on the wooden benches and pulpits of the church, exquisite manuscripts with impressively beautiful miniatures show how important a patron and employer the Church was for the artisan and artist of the Middle Ages. More intimate and exquisite was another product of convent and monastery life: mysticism. The passionate poems of Sister Hadewych (early 13th century) and the spiritual prose of Johan Ruusbroeck (1294 - 1381) are pinnacles in Dutch literature. It should be mentioned that for this pious literature the Dutch language was used. It had taken centuries before written Dutch was used: those who could read and write, the clergymen, originally used Latin as their writing language and this retarded the use of written Dutch. But in the 13th century the mystics, trying to express themselves as intimately as they could, started to use their own common language at the same time as, in laymen's circles, people started to write in Dutch.

Finally there is that remarkable wave of pious penance coupled with adventure which, again in the wake of the French example, worked itself out in the Low Countries: the Crusades (10th - 12th century). Many were the knights and their men, who, with papal blessing, set out from these parts on the Crusades to liberate the Holy Sepulchre from the hands of the Mohammedans. And whatever explanations one could find to explain the motives of the people who went, and they were certainly not all as lofty as they seemed (overpopulation, greed, struggle for power, need for adventure), it was on papal initiative and its justification had religious and ecclesiastic origins. Here again church life and church power was part and parcel of the general life and outlook of those times.

*Gouda's gothic Town Hall*

# 7        The rise of the cities

*13th - 15th century*

The revival of trade during the 13th and 14th centuries caused the rise of the cities in the Netherlands. Trade had never completely disappeared, but it had been much more sporadic and incidental, much more limited and restricted than previously. Instead of fairly irregular trade in various precious luxury articles which often had to be carried from far away and were of an exotic nature, utility and bulk goods became available in much better regulated market. The circulation of money, a powerful stimulus for the development of trade, increased. It is not improbable that the Crusades stimulated contacts with the Near East. At any rate the great Italian ports like Genoa and Venice gained enormous profits from friends and enemies in the Crusades. There was possibly a supply of gold from Africa which furthered the circulation of coined money. The increase in population throughout Europe is also held to be one of the causes of the revival of trade because of the need for larger supplies of foodstuffs. The growing taste for luxury among powerful kings and wealthy nobility must have stimulated the trade in jewels and spices, silk and weapons. Be that as it may, trade started to increase from

the Mediterranean, the Baltic area, Germany and England.
Many other countries in Europe acquired a profitable
share. In the Low Countries, Flanders in particular
developed a rich trade, but the northern territories of the
Netherlands joined with promising results.

In the Netherlands, trade had been resumed when the
invasions of the Danes were over, but at that time still at a
low level and on a small scale. Since the 10th century the
Frisian seafarers, thanks to their knowledge of the inland
waters and waterways, had built up new contacts for their
shipping and trade. New settlements such as Tiel and
Deventer took over the role of the vanished Frisian
colonization in Dorestad. But it was not long before Utrecht
once again became the central market for this reviving
trade. The counts of Gelre and Holland still abided by the
Frankish traditions of moving from one country seat to the
next to use up their revenues on the spot. The Bishop of
Utrecht, however, probably inspired by Roman and
ecclesiastical examples, chose Utrecht as his permanent
residence and the presence of ecclesiastical and
administrative officials required a steady supply of goods.
Utrecht's position was, until the 13th century, particularly
favourable for trade, though from then onwards ships
preferred the inland rivers and canals of Holland. Most of
the shipping during these earlier Middle Ages chose the
inland waters for sailing from the north to the south or vice
versa. In this way the skippers avoided the dangerous open
North Sea on their route from the Baltic along the Dutch
coast, finding their way across the Zuyder Zee, down the
Vecht and the Rhine towards Bruges, the leading trading
centre of Western Europe. The city of Dordrecht owed its
early development to this same inland route: its position
moreover allowed it to draw the shipping traffic between
the German hinterland and England. Dordrecht even
succeeded in getting the monopolistic right of staple: all
goods that came through the city had to be stored there
and were then traded by Dordrecht merchants. This offered
vast opportunities for bulk storage and speculative
contracts. Before this later development of Dordrecht in the
13th century, the towns along the IJssel and some towns on
the coast of the Zuyder Zee (Harderwijk, Elburg etc.) had
gained considerable importance. These towns had even

been able to join the larger trade union of the Baltic: the Hanseatic league. As Hanseatic cities Deventer, Zwolle and Kampen enjoyed profits from the Baltic route to the largest Hanseatic port in the west: Bruges. At a later period, after the rise of Dordrecht in the 13th century, other ports in the west, Amsterdam, Enkhuizen, Hoorn and Medemblik, were to get a share in the trade between the Baltic and Bruges, competing with the monopolistic Hansa.

But in the meantime the settlements had become cities and were essentially different from the former trade settlements such as Dorestad or Tiel. These older settlements had indeed been nothing more than unprotected, small collections of houses for the families of the (Frisian) merchants who themselves often travelled around in armed groups peddling their trade. With the expansion of trade and its regularization, the settlements also grew and finally became cities. The origin of such cities was in fact very old: they sometimes dated back to Roman times and were camps of strongholds then, others had been originally nothing more than small villages huddled together near castles and abbeys, and sometimes they had been just small marketplaces for the exchange of goods and agricultural products. Occasionally, entirely new spots were chosen as suitable for settlement - with an eye on traffic, near river and road crossings, near ports, or sometimes just because some landowner took the initiative. It is not certain to what extent the development of the real cities, which had at least to show an increase in the number of inhabitants, is due either to the influx of wandering merchants who decided to settle down and brought new life and more people to sleepy settlements, or to a slow internal development of the population itself, as a result of increasing prosperity, earlier marriage and increase in the birthrate. Opinions today tend to the latter interpretation. In general, the increase in population between the 11th and 13th centuries throughout Europe is an unexplained but established fact. Infanticide had been virtually stopped by the Church at a much earlier date, but it seems probable that economic expansion stimulated earlier marriage and that prosperity in some way or other might have resulted in an average greater chance of survival. Looked at from another angle, the growth in population stimulated economic expansion, and long distance trade was necessary to get the products into areas where certain minerals could not be found or there was need of bulk transport of food such as grain.

At any rate, the Netherlands in particular sustained a particularly impressive increase in population accompanied by economic expansion. The most striking aspect was a strong urbanization, only surpassed in its density and intensity by central and northern Italy and some typical trading areas like the Baltic coast, southern Germany, and of course Flanders and Brabant. These cities must certainly have drawn people from the surrounding countryside. Especially serfs and wandering artisans who hoped to find a living in the thriving town. Thus new communities, in Holland and Zeeland and also Utrecht, were formed, which called for new organizations. The merchants, hard-headed individuals as they often were, did not feel responsible to anyone and wished to rule their organizations according to their own views and interests. The feudal landowners, who usually had a keen eye for the profitable prospects of this development in the trade settlements, especially for the larger circulation of money, were willing enough to grant city rights to such settlements. These rights gave the cities their own separate position, for they implied that the lords ceded a great deal of their judicial and political powers to the burghers. The city received in this way its own town government, to be elected according to its own rules within the city itself, and this government of the city was granted the right to local legislation, for levying its own taxation and taking part in the courts of justice where the representative of the feudal lord was to remain the chairman. The construction of a surrounding earthen, later stone, wall symbolized the virtual isolation, the separate 'island' character within the still feudalized manorial countryside. Sometimes the feudal lords went even further: they granted privileges such as storage and staple rights, bans on the execution of certain crafts in the surrounding lands by which the cities could become centres of monopoly, subjecting the surrounding areas to their economic and even political power. The counts of Holland and Gelre even went so far as to promote the development of cities by granting city rights in advance, hoping that small villages and settlements such as Haarlem, Delft and Leiden would become real cities by these acts and grants (12th century). Some of these 'cities' never got further than the status of prosperous villages, proud of their title as a city but powerless to attain it: Purmerend, Edam, Beverwijk and Monnikendam.

Naturally the real, busy cities developed a richly varied social life. The rich, who mostly took over the city government and formed the exclusive patrician class within a city, were the leaders in every way and the truly powerful. Yet one should not have a poor opinion of the middle classes, the artisans and smaller tradespeople, who formed their own organizations (guilds) to defend themselves against competition from the outside and to maintain the standards of their own trade. And then there were the labouring class and the riff-raff that trickled constantly into the cities, fugitive serfs, peddlars and beggars, who supplied the labour in those cities, in particular where larger industries developed like the breweries in Haarlem, Gouda and Delft, the cloth mills in Leiden (14th century). These social conditions also held the danger of tension and struggle. Often the merchants formed a domineering clique, inaccessible to strangers, and developing into a select oligarchy. Towards the end of the Middle Ages the guilds tended to become very conservative institutions, killing every initiative, keeping prices up and violently persecuting and branding as interlopers other capable artisans, who for some reason or other did not belong to the guilds. The poorer classes were eventually no better off than the paupers in the country, whose situation could be miserable. And all these conditions became worse when times were bad and a city tended to decline economically. In flourishing cities, however, such tensions and deteriorations were hidden or even channelled by prosperity and hard work, by a show of buildings and expansion. The dynamic influence of money helped to create for most cities the possibility of growth and expansion.

In medieval Netherlands the rise of the cities was indeed a dynamic element of great importance. Trade and transport stimulated rapid growth in this geographically so favourably situated delta. The counterweight of a strong aristrocracy or a powerful monarch was absent. The countryside soon became economically dependent on the cities and the smaller landowners adapted themselves to these realities. The virtual liberation of the rural areas was, as a consequence, the indirect result of the presence of the cities. Through the circulation of money many serfs could pay their ransom to their lords. They often agreed on a lease with their money-loving lords, which freed them of all oppressive duties and services. Escaped serfs could gain freedom inside the cities if they managed to stay there for a certain period. In this way the free farmer, formerly a serf on his small plot of land, tried to improve his production on that same plot of land which he now leased. During the 12th century these small farmers started to fertilize their land and to improve their crops. Land reclamation from the peat bogs also contributed to the liberation of serfs and caused an increase of agrarian production.

Cities also helped in liberating the mind. The individual enterprising spirit of the merchant, relying upon his own wit and abilities, made him more independent of the authority of the Church. The management of his affairs compelled him to learn reading, writing and arithmetic. This broke the cultural monopoly of the clergy and the foundations were laid of a lay culture, of a secularization of the mind. It implied that this culture became more worldly minded, less impregnated by religion and piety. The interest in stories as such, of knight and romantic adventures, was typical of the new taste of the burghers. Typical also was their preference for their own language - with them Latin had priority no longer. Thus an independent Dutch literature started to develop in the 13th century, and not just as a result of the outbursts of the mystics mentioned before. Here again Flanders took the lead: Jacob van Maerlandt (1235 - 1295) was to be the first great Dutch translator and author. 'Renard the Fox' was one of the first popular stories recorded in the Dutch language. All over the Netherlands, guilds for poetry and rhetorics were founded, societies where people, mostly wealthy burghers, gathered to exercise their talent for poetry, writing and eloquence. A good example illustrating the secularization of culture is the change that took place in the dramatic arts. Drama, which started as mystery plays performed in the church to illustrate biblical stories, took a livelier acting with angels and devils, and farce became a popular entertainment. Drama literally moved out of the church - performances first given in the building of the church in front of the altar, were moved to the large porch at the entrance and finally to the church square.

*Philip the Good of Burgundy*

# 8    Burgundy

*15th century*

France and England led the way and the Low Countries
followed. The smaller, independent sovereignties of counts
and dukes and bishops were gradually amalgamated
until this united collection of feudal states could finally be
governed more efficiently from one central point. This in
fact involved some kind of centralization and the rise of one
monarchic power. Why did this happen in the Low
Countries especially during the 14th and 15th centuries?
Was it owing to the increasing use and circulation of
money, or to the closer contacts of trade and traffic among
the different counties, or to the rise of the cities in earlier
times that weakened the power of the local aristocracy? Or
was it perhaps because the more efficiently minded,
practical patrician of the city favoured a more reasonable
and coherent system of government? Or was it on the
other hand due to the economic recession which struck
particularly severely in other countries during the 14th
century, where a decrease of the population was apparent,
and probably had its influence in the Low Countries as
well? Coincidences may have played a major role in the
Low Countries: perhaps the English and especially French

examples of centralized power were of vital importance. The extinction of certain ruling families in the male line could not have been foreseen, although such a risk had realistically been taken into account and a scheme of marriage policy had strengthened the bond between the different families and guaranteed some sort of secure succession even if extinction in the male line should take place. Double marriages between two children - a daughter and a son - of one family and two of another family were often planned by the Habsburgs to strengthen the bonds between them and other reigning dynasties. Alii pugnant, tu felix Austria nube - others have to fight for it, but you, happy Austria, only have to marry. It was in this way that at the end of the 15th century the Habsburgs entered the line of succession in the Low Countries also.

This final mammoth fusion had, however, been preceded by gradual unification within the Netherlands under one ruling family. The family tree of the Counts of Holland (and Zeeland) could be used to illustrate what happened. In 1299 the title of Holland was inherited by the Counts of Hainault, and both titles eventually passed to the Duke of Burgundy (1433). This Duke of Burgundy had started on the ladder to success as a French vassal. Through marrying into the line of the Counts of Flanders he acquired that title (1405), to which the dukedom of Brabant and that of Limburg were soon added. When finally the bishoprics of Liege and Utrecht were also held by relatives of the family of Burgundy, many strings were held in one hand. The energetic Burgundian sovereign who assembled all these different counties under one banner was Philip the Good (1419 - 1467). Philip had deliberately planned this union, with all his talents for ruling, tact and intrigue, sometimes even by force of arms, but he was helped by nature too: the mortality rate was high even in aristocratic families and the extinction of many families in the male line seemed to be unavoidable.

When at last Philip the Good had all the strings in hand - a collection of counties assembled in one personal union - he wanted to pull these strings and that implied centralization. It was by no means an easy job. After all, Philip the Good was not King of one coherent collection of territories with a traditional capital and residence in its centre: he was still count of one province, duke of another and his relation to each region was restricted by special rights and privileges as varied as the dukedoms, counties and bishoprics. The resistance of nobility and burghers on a local and regional scale had to be broken. The work was carried out - cautiously by Philip, impetuously by his son Charles the Bold (1467 - 1477), but never reached a final phase of complete centralization. Roman law came to the aid of royal power - civic judges of burgher origin gave their support. In the courts of the sovereigns an officialdom was formed to initiate and control the measures required by these attempts at central government. A Grand Council was founded which functioned as a central advisory body to the Lord of the Low Countries, who as a Duke of Burgundy had collected so many other titles. A Parliament was founded in Malines to serve as the supreme court of justice to the entire country, and about 1464 the different regions started to send their representatives to an assembly, sporadically called together by the Lord of the Low Countries, which had to decide on special grants required by him in cases of emergency (the Estates General). After 1477, with the sudden death of Charles the Bold, a relapse set in. His only daughter and successor, whose position was extremely weak, had to give up a large part of her power to local patricians and aristocrats. Once she had found support by marrying Maximilian of Habsburg, the old policy of centralization could slowly be taken up again. Brussels gradually became the residence of these princes, and international relations through the Habsburgs at last gave the house of Burgundy that final glory it seemed to need to become a real centralized monarchy.

The Burgundian ideas of unity were modern and progressive for their times: the loose arrangements with the disintegrating autonomous power of the cities on the one hand and local aristocrats on the other seemed to have had its day, and in particular the decadence of an already weakened nobility seemed to point to the Burgundian solution. It became Burgundian tactics to draw these aristocrats into service as courtiers near the throne, and the burghers as officials and lawyers in the service of the councils and departments. It is curious that with this slow and certain decline of the old nobility and knighthood, the glorification of knights and their honour should dominate a large part of the Burgundian court culture. Leading authors such as Froissard, de Commynes, Chastellain portrayed this great past, which to them was very much alive, in a light which the 20th century historian Huizinga later interpreted as the glow of gold and brown of autumn rather than the brilliant colour of summer. The gold, perhaps, dominated. The Burgundian court favoured a pomp and circumstance which was intended to obscure the aura of knights and noble-men. Sometimes this pomp was crude and vulgar, but it could be great and magnificent, in particular in the promotion of fine arts, a typical example of court patronage, which encouraged painters who were commissioned to paint portraits on linen or in books. The court also made rich donations to churches, where once again painters and craftsmen could do their work, and there were magnificent miniatures (often with decorated lettering) in preciously written manuscripts. Great painters such as the Van Eyck brothers (d. 1426 and 1441) and Memlinc (d. 1494) and Claus Sluter the sculptor (d. 1406) were given chances to express themselves which they used to the full.

The centre of culture at this time was in the southern Netherlands, the north only basked in the glow. The Burgundian court itself was entirely French in language, fashion and tradition. Inevitably this French influence worked its way into the culture of the Netherlands, yet the fine arts bore a Duth individuality, a sober sense of reality and realism combined with a serene kind of intimacy, which were typical. The north reflected so to say the radiation of the south: Dirk Bouts (d. 1475) came from Haarlem to be taught by Jan van Eyck, and fifty years later the Dutch painter Gerard David (d. 1523) set out for Bruges. Even the works of the great artists who stayed would have been unthinkable without the influence of the south: Hieronymus Bosch (d. 1516) of 's-Hertogenbosch, the painter of the miraculous and the weird, can only be understood in the light of his congeniality with what was done in Flanders and the other cities of Brabant, and Pieter Breughel (1525 - 1569) was perhaps in many respects his pupil and follower.

Without the influence of the Southern Netherlands' religious movements of the 13th century, the Northern Netherlands' movement of Modern Devotion of the 15th century cannot be understood either. Geert Grote (1340 - 1384) had absorbed many of Ruusbroeck's thoughts before the launched his own movement of renewal through preaching and in particular by the foundation of a circle of congenial clergy in Deventer and Zwolle. The similarity of the Dutch and Lower German languages contributed towards the unity and speedy propagation of this movement, and all over the Low Countries and West Germany monasteries accepted the rules Geert Grote had set. Typical of this movement were the practical worldly views of the 'Brothers of the Common Life', who at the same time displayed a remarkable intellectual eagerness in the pursuit of the sciences, shown by a great interest in copying books and writing manuscripts, thus making them available in the monastic libraries. There was also a strong tendency to return to truly pious living, through the fulfillment of clearly determined duties, through the deepening of individual faith and through the propagation of devotional, edifying preaching. There were interesting contacts with laymen, when they tried to show them the simple but important prescripts of a pious life. The movements bore rich fruits such as the famous 'Imitatio Christi', probably written by Thomas à Kempis (1380 - 1471); Erasmus, the famous humanist, was educated in one of the monasteries of the movement.

The seeds of Humanism and Reformation were sown and took root in the fertile soil of the Modern Devotion movement, when this movement itself began to decline. It is not correct perhaps to draw direct lines from this movement forward to the 16th century, but it had to a limited extent been influential, and it indicated what thoughts and beliefs had begun to develop within and without the Church.

# Humanists, anabaptists and Calvinists

*16th century*

During the first half of the 16th century, events in the Church and religion overshadowed political developments. Charles the Bold's grandson, Charles V (1516 - 1555), continued the policy of centralization, and his realm was rounded off by the conquests of Friesland (1524), Groningen (1536) and Gelre (1543). Resistance of particularly powerful and selfwilled cities was punished, as in the case of Ghent, and the bonds with the Holy Roman Empire were regulated in such a way that the Low Countries from then on were considered one whole, and their relationship with the highest feudal lord, the Emperor, was practically, though not formally, ended. Charles V, as a descendant of the house of Habsburg, was heir not just to the very important and rich lands in the Low Countries, but also to the throne of Spain and the princedoms in Austria, and was also elected Emperor in Germany. Politically the Netherlands were added in this way to that magic chain of powerful titles which made the Habsburgs wielders of world power. When Charles V resigned in 1555, both the Low Countries and Spain remained under one head, although he had been wise enough not to pass the German

Imperial crown and the Austrian heriditary territories to his son Philip II (ruled 1555 - 1581; in Spain - 1598).

Perhaps the accidental union of Spain and the Low Countries under one ruler would not have caused such problems if the politics of Philip II had not been swept into the maelstrom of other events. The Reformation placed Charles V and Philip II in immense internal and external conflicts and strife. From the very beginning in 1517 the influence of Lutheranism could be discerned in the Low Countries, although the number of real followers had not been large. The writings of Luther, however, and the translations of the Bible entered the country very soon and must have affected some groups in the population immediately. In particular in such trading and shipping ports as Antwerp merchants were soon in contact with the new heresies, and the propagation of these new ideas was facilitated by the newly invented art of printing. This new technique resulted in a rapid increase in the number of books and pamphlets. The Reformation was a movement in print: many printing offices were set up in the Low Countries, traditional centres for trade and traffic, which did a great deal to spread its ideas. Although Lutheranism gave the initial impetus, Dutch development was to lake a different turn.

The spiritual movement which partly prepared and partly coincided with the Reformation was Humanism. This humanism should not be seen exclusively in the light of the Reformation. Many humanists not only did not intend the rupture in the Church, but when it came they refused to accept it. They were in favour rather of a kind reformation and purification within the Church. In many ways inspired by the Modern Devotion they tried to tap sources older than the medieval pious and religious ones which were the inspiration for the 'Brothers of the Common Life'. These sources they found in antiquity, especially in the pagan Roman authors of classical literature, and in their ideas they believed they had found more wisdom and perspicacity, above all more real purity in the expression of logical and social-moralistic thought. This search for purity also led them back to the Bible, in which they searched for the true message in plain words, undiluted by the later commentaries and explanations of the scholars of the

Middle Ages. An intensive correspondence, often published, united the humanists of all countries in Christian Europe.

In the Netherlands, Erasmus (1476 - 1536) was to be the greatest humanist of them all. The fact that he neither sided with the Reformation nor followed the lead of counter-reformatory popes, was not an act of cowardice. His writings, such as the famous satirical tract 'Laus Stultitiae' bear witness to a brave spirit which did not flinch in the face of supreme power, nor did he avoid the issues at stake. His editions of ancient authors and Bible texts testify to his zeal and devotion for the real purification of church and belief. Erasmus rejected the Reformation because he wanted to preserve the unity of western Christianity, but he condemned just as strongly the Roman Catholic Counter Reformation because he believed in toleration and frankness, in a way of life based on the simple principles of Christian humanity rather than on strict doctrinal rules and regulations. In this manner humanism paved the way for the Reformation without identifying itself: it was the outlook of a small but very influential elite of scholars and intellectuals, often close to the thrones of princes and prelates, important 'bestselling' authors for a wider public of burghers and nobles.

Altogether different was the atmosphere in which the real Reformation appeared in the Netherlands in a more intensive way. All of a sudden and with rapid succes there spread a heretical belief of anabaptism from 1530 onwards. It had a following of ecstatic, revolutionary people, carried away by a firm belief in the imminent return of Christ. It found many adherents in the north of the Netherlands and in areas along the frontiers with Germany. It was a radical message which seemed to appeal to the intellectually weak and perhaps also to the socially destitute. The Middle Ages had known weird forms of mass exaltation: dancing frenzies, processions of flagellants, etc. and here the same fanatism driven on by millenarian ideas occurred again. In bitter cold, anabaptists ran around stark naked in the streets of Amsterdam, prophesying the end of the world, and at one of their meetings it could happen that a member, carried away by his own ecstasy, would put a piece of red-hot coal in his mouth. This excessive fanatism finally drove people from Holland, Friesland and Brabant to the one city, Münster, where they were to await the coming of the Lord, and where the new Jerusalem would be built. Their leader, an artisan named Jan van Leyden, could not hold out against a siege by hired troops of the bishop of Münster, and in the summer of 1535 the city was captured. Anabaptism was to collapse in a violent orgy of murder and executions in a starving city, but it would not disappear altogether. Many adherents had stayed at home: and these quiet baptists, under the leadership of the Frisian preacher Menno Simonsz (1496 - 1559), kept in touch with each other and developed a secret church community which held radical Christian views but had dropped the millenarian conviction of the immediate return of Christ. Often they would clash with the authorities, who, remembering anabaptist violence, feared their heresies and could easily identify them because they refused to take an oath or carry arms. These baptists were called Mennonites (or 'Doopsgezinden') and were to play their own role in the later protestantism of the Netherlands.

It was obvious, however, that more advanced doctrine, a better church organization and a more realistic outlook would be needed to give protestantism real impetus. The teachings of the Frenchman John Calvin (1509 - 1564) were radical enough - strict, logical and consequent. Calvinism was less exclusively intellectual than humanism, less unrealistic and sectarian than anabaptism. God's absolute power and greatness made man a humble, sinful creature, but the chance of receiving grace and the possibility of honouring God by serving him in daily toil, gave the faithful almost unlimited strength and courage. The awareness of sin saved them from apathy and selfsufficiency. A strong believe in the absolute truth of Calvin's views encouraged the idea that rulers who suppressed this True Religion were godless tyrants who could eventually be deposed. Calvinist organization was attractive too: although in principle giving equal rights to all members, a smaller group of elders together with the minister kept matters firmly in hand. From Geneva, the city where Calvin was finally able to found his Church, the message penetrated through France to the Low Countries. Once again it must have been originally the lawless and the destitute who first fixed their hopes on this radical doctrine, and in particular in the large Flemish cities the new Calvinist religion found many adherents from 1550 onwards. Soon it spread to other classes, to other areas. It suited the intellectuals because of the highly sophisticated writings of Calvin, it suited the artisans because of its glorification of labour as good in the eyes of God. Discipline, religious conviction, radicalism, strict dogmatism gave Calvinism its power in the Low Countries, where the official government had rejected the Reformation, and both Lutheranism and anabaptism had failed to hold their followers.

The public authorities, dreading more than anything religious dissension at a time when they were working to achieve political unity, did all they could to suppress heresy. Ever since 1523 victims had died for their faith. But the blood of these martyrs was the seed for the new church. From 1550 the more intensive persecutions of heretics created increasing unrest with the population. Magistrates and clergymen objected to severe punishments of heretics, common people often felt sympathy with the poor man who was burned at the stake. Resistance rose everywhere: heretics were liberated from prison by mob violence, images of the saints (which to the Calvinists was idolatry) were besmirched and destroyed, and after 1560 Calvinists began to demonstrate openly for their faith by singing religious hymns in processions and by organizing open-air meetings. All this helped to make the Low Countries in the 1560s an increasingly restive and restless country, causing a great deal of alarm in the governmental centre at Brussels.

# 10    The outbreak of the Revolt

*(1566)*

Many are the causes of the insurrection which broke out in
1566 in a wave of iconoclasm. The religious overtones of this
rebellion became clear with its first actions: the smashing
of religious images in the churches. The severe religious
persecutions during the reigns of Charles and Philip II had
caused unrest and resistance. Especially was this the case
after 1560 when riots occurred everywhere, which the
authorities had not been able to control. The smashing of
images, however, had not much in common with these
previous minor riots. The storm broke first in the extreme
south of Flanders, and swept across the Netherlands until it
spent itself a few months later in the north of Leeuwarden.
During the more or less systematic and organized
smashing of images, riotous crowds would surge through
the streets, bent on violence and destruction, particularly in
southern cities. It is not improbable that Calvinist leaders,
noblemen and rich merchants sometimes encouraged and
organized the iconoclasm, and in some areas the ruling
nobility or city magistrates undertook an orderly removal of
the images from the churches, as happened with
Brederode in Vianen. It is also possible that some citizens

of rank, afraid of having their own homes and warehouses looted, encouraged the rebellious groups to plunder the churches - which at any rate was safer for them. In any case images in churches were considered by Calvinists as idolatrous heathenism and they certainly championed a 'cleansing' of the houses of God in this way.

Yet such iconoclasm was also a consequence of the social and economic situation. Why otherwise should there be a need for diverting the populace from looting the houses and warehouses of the rich? Why were Roman Catholics themselves sometimes willing to risk their necks to air their fury against the Church? Undoubtedly, there existed a strong feeling of anti-clericalism, which criticized in particular the parasitical way of life of the clergy, and blamed the high prelates for all the evils of the world. War with France had caused misery and poverty among the less fortunate, when rising wages had just given them a taste for better living. Epidemics and bad harvests, severe winters and floods easily stimulated unrest among those who lived on the edge of subsistance level anyway. Prices of grain had risen at a terrifying rate, as a result of difficulties with supplies from the Baltic, especially during the years of 1565 and 1566.

There were also political reasons behind these events which could not be overlooked. It is not surprising that Philip II, hearing of the outbreaks of iconoclasm, immediately thought of the responsibility of noblemen and rich burghers rather than just of heretics and rebels of the lower classes. Those very circles had voiced such severe criticism in previous years: their political grievances against the régime of King Philip and his governors in the Low Countries were so deep that they had repeatedly expressed their dissatisfaction in open protests and demonstrations. They had a growing feeling of unease about the policy of centralization directed by King Philip II from his residence in Spain and carried out by his officials in Brussels. City governments felt that they were losing many of their rights and privileges, the high and mighty position of the landowning nobility seemed to be undermined by the bureaucrats and officials in Brussels, local clergy felt that a stronger centralized church organization was usurping local powers. Clever politicians, jurists and officials, such as Granvelle and Viglius, indeed tried to draw the management of county and church affairs into the orbit of central government as much as possible, within the limits of existing traditions and rights. A Secret Council, steering clear of the Grand Council (Raad van State), in which the nobility still occupied a relatively strong position, helped to give them room for such manoeuvres. The seemingly permanent presence of foreign mercenaries, paid and commanded directly from Brussels, had caused so much alarm that the government in Brussels had been forced to withdraw them temporarily in 1564 only to call them back once more after the iconoclastic outbreak. Religious persecutions and the unrest they caused among the population of all classes created a very realistic background to this political opposition. Did not such persecutions, directed from the centre, prove the intolerable and even inhuman meddling in local and regional affairs by faraway bureaucrats and fanatical zealots?

Finally, there must have existed feelings of a national or regional kind which clashed with aspects of Philip's reign which were considered to be 'foreign'. Philip II, although 'natural' ruler as Lord of the Low Countries, was more interested in his Kingdom in Spain and his war against the Turks in the Mediterranean and the French King, traditional enemies of the Habsburgs. Since 1560 he had chosen the Escorial in Spain for his residence, which greatly hindered the smooth functioning of his Brussels government, as he became a foreigner to his subjects in the Low Countries in this way. Foreign also were a number of officials of the Crown, often of Spanish, Italian or French origin without any natural, that is to say inherited, territorial or traditional rights like other cosmopolitan high nobles. Foreign also were the mercenary troops stationed in the country, never very popular in their garrison cities; so were the modernistic attemps at centralization, at streamlining church government, at making taxation more efficient, at persecuting and killing heretics in a more systematic way. All this explains why the iconoclasm was in fact a form of relief for many existing tensions, in itself a mixture of religious, economic and social, political and cultural elements; a relief, however, which was a sore disillusion not only to those who supported the policies of Brussels but also to those who were more or less guilty themselves, the more moderate opposition of the leading noblemen and burghers. This kind of destructive and plebeian rebellion had never been intended by the leaders of the opposition. Had some form of a rebellion been unavoidable, an organized kind of war under the leadership of knightly noblemen or a league of defenders of rights and privileges should have been waged against the tyrannical government in Brussels, on the pattern of the Huguenot party in France. But after the outbreak many noblemen offered their services to the government in Brussels in order to punish the instigators and re-establish what they considered to be order. Nevertheless, unrest was caused by the iconoclasm which did not simmer down very quickly. Calvinist bands, reinforced by downtrodden nobles and paupers, rambled through the country even trying to seize certain cities. When these attacks failed - they succeeded at first in capturing Valenciennes - they withdrew to the woods or the sea. These 'beggars' (Geuzen) then provided for themselves by pilfering and looting on land (boschgeuzen) or by privateering (watergeuzen). Their failure to bring about any positive change except for destruction and economic blockading, was chiefly due to the interference of the order-loving nobility and magistrates.

The entire insurrection might have ended as another intermezzo, perhaps as shortlived as the anabaptist movement of thirty years before, had not Philip II, after delays due to difficulties of communication over such a distance and his own slackness, wanted things otherwise. Severely and methodically he wished to extinguish the smouldering fire of opposition and resistance, to punish not only those who had actually smashed the images or tried to follow up the iconoclasm with military actions, but also the moderate opposition of noblemen and magistrates who had supported the Brussels government in order to prevent civil war. A faithful servant to the Spanish throne, the Duke of Alba, was sent to the Low Countries to restore real order for good and all, not sparing the opposition forces of high noblemen and wealthy citizens.

It was at this moment that the insurrection of 1566, although widely but weakly spread, flaring up here and there to die out again at once, developed into a real revolt or even revolution, in fact into a war which started with frontier skirmishes and local unrest and finally swept across the country in real campaigns, sieges and battles. This war was to last for eighty years - though interrupted by an armistice of twelve years (1609 - 1621) and by periods of relative quiet. Instead of making use of the fear which iconoclasm had caused in the moderate opposition of citizens and noblemen, Philip II upset the move towards local co-operation with Brussels by his unexpected and severe decision to send Alba. Especially after the flight of William of Orange things took a turn which neither Alba nor Philip had foreseen. This noblemen of high rank planned his flight as a temporary retreat, in order to strike with greater strength: he had at last decided to lead a real rebellion and to accept the inevitable development of a civil war.

William of Orange, a German count of Nassau by birth (1533) had by whimsical fate become heir to the richest properties in the Low Countries (Baronet of Breda) and at the same time to the sovereign principality of Orange, an enclave in the Kingdom of France. This put him at once on a level with the highest nobility in the Low Countries and with the ruling kings and princes of his time. Educated for this very reason at the court of Brussels, he became thoroughly familiar with the problems of his new country, and with his keen intelligence he soon discovered that for the nobility times were not favourable - he saw that all the important decisions of government tended to be taken over the heads of the nobles whom he considered to be the 'natural' leaders of the people. This challenged him to step forward as the leader of the moderate opposition and to get in touch with what there was of unrest and fermentation among the population. Although he still wanted to serve the official Roman Catholic Church, his German origin gave him sympathies towards Lutheranism and he certainly did not want to antagonize the heretics by severe persecutions and fanatical intolerance. His own belief, though still Catholic, was that of a practical Christian in the sense that he believed in tolerant and morally decent conduct. When, at the end of 1664, he voiced dissatisfaction about the religious persecutions, this protest, at least for himself, was more than just that of an opposition leader trying to put pressure on the government by any means. For a long time he tried to prevent the civil war he saw coming and his tolerant spirit was horrified by the mass breaking of images. In Antwerp he restored order by force of arms and it seemed that he had reverted to being a servant of the centralizing government in Brussels after all. However, his keen political insight persuaded him to leave the country when he heard of the appointment of Alba. He realized that in this way Philip II was also attacking the moderate opposition, and that from then on there would be no room for his ideals of tolerance.

Was this decision of William of Orange, one may ask, of such great significance? The answer would be in the negative if, after his decision, William of Orange had considered his career finished and gone back to his German family to wait quietly until he could regain his rich properties from the hands of the legal ruler of the Low Countries, Philip II. More political and economic considerations would have prompted such a decision. But his idealism showed him a different path, and he took a decision, which was not an easy one to take, which led to higher and greater causes. He did not want to wait and see if the situation, unfavourable to him personally, would change: he wished to return, not humbly asking for his property, but as the leader of all those in the Low Countries who awaited protection of their rights and privileges ('liberty') and hoped for tolerance towards those who held a different Christian belief but were obedient and quiet subjects.

# 11    The formation of the Republic

*1568 - 1609*

Alba tried to restore order with a firm, severe hand and
continued the policy of centralization. In this, however, he
worked slowly and cautiously. He introduced a heavy
and modern tax system (the so-called 'tithe') which was to
take effect in all counties and which would have been fairer
to rich and poor alike than the old system with unjust local
variations and heavy pressure on the poor through indirect
taxation. Vigorous protest caused delay, and the long civil
war shelved the whole idea. William of Orange tried to stir
up trouble in the country itself by means of military
assaults, but his expeditions spent themselves through lack
of funds, hesitations and especially because of the weak
response from the population. But he did not give up, and
by 1572 he had made new plans and assembled his
mercenary troops once more. He got in touch with the
privateering sea-beggars who still infested the North Sea
and hoped for aid from the French protestant party of the
Huguenots. Curiously enough, this time more people within
the country joined him. In some cities resistance was
stirred up by a few nobles and some magistrates and others
followed suit. Many were persuaded in the end by hatred of

the foreign troops which had returned with Alba; others by fear of the privateers who were admitted to some towns if they promised to spare the population; and a few dared to side with William because Alba was not able to have his troops everywhere, and himself was badly hampered by lack of funds. The little city of Den Briel, where the sea-beggars suddenly landed on 1 April 1572, gave the lead: the privateers were admitted within the walls and the weak Spanish garrison thrown out. Other towns followed suit: Rotterdam, Flushing, Dordrecht, Enkhuizen, Hoorn, Haarlem, Gouda and Leiden.

The people who sided with the rebels were certainly not all fanatic Calvinists, although the latter often took the lead. In Flushing, for instance, townsfolk marched to the town hall to compell the city fathers to hoist the sea-beggars' flag - after having heard Mass! Not until some time after the changes in these towns did the Calvinist minorities grow bolder. They claimed the big churches and dismissed the outspoken Roman Catholics who had stayed, out of the government, arguing that they were not trustworthy in the pursuit of the Cause. They closed monasteries and convents, 'purified' the churches of all 'idolatrous' symbols and finally succeeded in prohibiting Catholic public worship. From then onwards a process of 'protestantization' set in. Most public professions and occupations became available to protestants only, schools were put under Protestant supervision, magistrates were expected to be Protestant themselves. After a lapse of two of three generations, Calvinist minorities had become majorities. More members were brought to the new Church by pressure and compulsion than by true conversion.

Why did all this happen with such striking force in Holland and Zeeland and not elsewhere, especially since Calvinism had been much more powerful in Flanders and Brabant than in the north? Perhaps it was a matter of distance from Brussels and of the relative isolation of these sea provinces which helped to keep a rebellion going, which had been quickly squashed in 1566 in Flanders. Holland and Zeeland had suffered most from the raids of the privateering sea-beggars since 1566 and the Dutch shipping trade had been barred from many an important sea-route. The difficult communications over the great rivers and in the delta gave Holland and Zeeland time to consolidate their rebellion. This was also proved by further failures of William of Orange's planned campaign in the south, notwithstanding the fact that feelings towards him had improved and Malines, for example, had opened its gates for his troops at once. Alba struck back fast, thus saving the threatened position of Brussels.

Orange had enough sense of strategy and tactics to switch immediately to Holland when his original plans to spread the rebellion through the country failed. He had himself re-appointed by the rebel government of the cities in Holland (the provincial estates) to his former position of Stadtholder of Holland and Zeeland - a task which had been a military and governing function within a province representing the governor of the Low Countries. He came over to Holland, settling finally in Delft, and when he realized that the Calvinists were the driving force behind the successfull rebellion, joined the new Church. From Holland as his base he hoped to bring all the provinces of the Low Countries under the banner of the insurrection. He expected that within these territories as a whole Roman Catholics and Calvinists would exist side by side respecting each other's churches. The power of the Calvinists in Holland and Zeeland seemed to be irresistible, but further resistance in other provinces would only be possible if the Catholics were guaranteed complete freedom of religion, as a condition of joining in. In this respect William's ideal of tolerance seemed to be supported by realistic political aims.

The arrival of the Prince of Orange in rebellious Holland was an inspiration to the people. The dashing, rich nobleman, educated in the brilliance of the Burgundian-Habsburgian court at Brussels, adapted himself to the simple and rough atmosphere of this province of merchants and magistrates. He became an austere and dignified, modest personality who seemed to be influenced by the strict Calvinist outlook without ever losing his ideal of bringing together all the Dutch provinces in one federation of states, where differences of belief would be unimportant because of the Christian need for unity despite dogmatic differences.

Holland indeed was in urgent need of inspired leadership.

Alba finally sent a punitive expedition to the north to suppress the rebels in the Dutch cities of Holland once and for all. William of Orange was able to persuade the city magistrates to resist and not to capitulate. Several cities kept their gates shut and had to stand a siege. The city of Haarlem, despite a brave defence, had to capitulate (1572-3). Alkmaar was saved for the rebels by the flooding of surrounding polders (1573) and Leiden, overcome by starvation and exhaustion in a terrible siege, was finally liberated with the aid of William's troops aided by sea-beggars who rallied to the town across flooded land in flat-bottomed boats (3 October 1574). The world marvelled at the courage of these small Dutch towns in watery Holland who dared to resist the King whose realm was worldwide. It appeared that the Spanish colossus had feet of clay. Sea-beggars and townpeople knocked the colossus down. Neither Alba nor his successors ever succeeded again in subjecting Holland or Zeeland.

Would Holland now be able to draw the other counties into the rebellion? The big chance came in 1576. The death of the governor who had succeeded the disillusioned Alba, had caused such a devastating mutiny among the Spanish mercenary troops, that the other counties were prepared to join in with Holland. They all agreed to petition the King for the withdrawal of foreign troops and the granting of freedom of religion as desired by each county. Holland and Zeeland were to remain Calvinist, the other counties tended to opt for Catholicism. Great were the days of William of Orange's triumphant return to Brussels, but this glory was not to last long. The revolutionary movement towards protestantization which had taken place in Holland and Zeeland did not develop in the south. Those who under Alba's government had often grumbled but never taken action, remained in power. For them the new agreement with the rebels in the north had been a convenient but temporary way of overcoming the untenable situation of 1576. Many were prepared to negotiate with their legal ruler, the Lord of the Netherlands, who was at the same time King of Spain. If Philip II was willing to make reasonable concessions towards the reestablisment of order while respecting the traditional rights of nobles and cities, things could take a turn for the better. The

Calvinists, who had fled after 1566 and now returned to the south, had cherished hopes of being welcomed as real liberators. But even in Ghent where they took over power, they met with a considerable resistance and remained in power only by tyrannical measures: a Calvinist dictatorship which spoilt a great deal of goodwill in the south towards the rebellion in general. William of Orange's ideal of a peaceful coexistence of Catholicism and Protestantism came to nothing.

This does not mean that William alone held these ideas. Such trends of thought had been international since the time of Erasmus, and found support in many circles of noblemen and intellectuals. In France it was the 'politiques' who looked for the same solution in their country as William hoped to find for the Low Countries. Dirck Volckertsz. Coornhert (1522 - 1590) was one of the passionate propagators of the supreme ideal of tolerance, as Castellio had defended such ideas in Switzerland and Italy. The wealthy merchants and burghers in the Dutch cities were often fundamentally tolerant towards different religions and were not merely thinking of their own economic interests in respecting the beliefs of others, whether Catholic, Calvinist or Lutheran. They often felt strongly about the basic truth of Christianity and the Christian way of life as such, and hated theological squabbles. In the heat of the insurrection, however, belligerent radicals had been more emphatic than the cautious moderates. In spite of all his efforts, William of Orange could not manage to bridge the gap between opinions, and in order to avoid any suggestions of centralization it was impossible for him to force all parties into the direction he desired. Thus the temporary union of the rebels of the north with the rebels in the south remained a loose federation of different groups with quite different plans and ideals. A capable governor like Alexander Farnese, Duke of Parma (from 1578), could exploit this internal dissension in favour of his King. He persuaded many counties, noblemen and magistrates in the south to return to the fold, and using the south as his base he started conquering the other provinces.

Times were hard for those who wanted to save the rebellion: a new agreement between those who remained faithful to the Cause could not save the situation (the Union of Utrecht, 1579). Parma advanced and occupied ever greater parts of the territories which legally belonged to his King. Groningen, Drente and Overijssel submitted again in 1580. And the centre of the rebellion, Holland and Zeeland, seemed once more to be thrown back upon its own resources and its own Stadtholder William of Orange.

In this situation of polarization within the Low Countries, between the original rebels of Holland and Zeeland on the one hand and the more Catholic regions in other provinces, a certain hardening of the Cause became discernible. Symbolic of this development was not only the special agreement of the Union of Utrecht, in which rebel provinces promised each other to keep together and to share the burdens of the war but also the Act of Deposition of the Lord of the Low Countries, Philip II (1581). This revolutionary act would gradually be considered of immense historical significance, because official obedience towards the God-given ruler was such an ingrained belief that even the misconduct of such a ruler could not be an excuse for deposing him. For a long time the rebels had stated officially that they were not fighting their natural ruler Philip, the legal count of Holland and Zeeland, but only his erring advisers. Only with the help of a new protestant theory which came from France, where the victories and slaughters by the Catholic Party had driven the Huguenot party into a most difficult situation, could the rebels in Holland finally formulate a firm reason to depose their ruler. Stating that in theory a natural ruler was bound by an unwritten contract with his people by which he had the duty to be a protector and not a tyrant, that is to say, a shepherd to his sheep, the rebels pronounced that they deposed their ruler because he had broken the contract unilaterally. This theory put for the first time into state practice, was in fact a daring justification of a real act of rebellion and the document of this Act of Deposition became so to say the mainspring of many later acts of rebellion also (e.g. in Cromwell's time and during the War of Independence of North America).

But documents did not help the rebels to hold off the enemy. William of Orange died by the hands of a fanatical murderer, who believed his act would please God (1584).

Antwerp fell in the same year, Parma captured Brussels one year later. Perhaps even Holland would not have been able to resist Parma's clever strategy, if natural conditions had not served as a helpful protection to the south and east, if Holland had not found two eminent leaders: Maurice, a son of William of Orange, who became a great general, and van Oldenbarnevelt, a clever statesman.

On the death of Parma (1591) the tide had already turned in favour of the rebels. In 1588 a gigantic Spanish invasion fleet, headed for England, had been scattered with the aid of the Dutch and was later completely destroyed by a terrible storm. Maurice's reconquests of strongholds and cities in the eastern provinces of Gelre and Overijssel had started in 1590. It was essential for the defence of the provinces of Holland and Utrecht that a defence-line along the river IJssel should be built up to hold off any possible attack from the east. By Maurice's operations and expeditions the 'Garden of Holland' on that side could be closed off. In the south Maurice reached, step by step, city by city, the mouth of the Scheldt, but Antwerp could not be recovered. When the armistice was signed in 1609 the Low Countries were actually torn apart and the continuation of the struggle after 1621 could not heal the breach. The south was back under the power of the Habsburgs and the north now constituted a separate, independent Republic.

The formation of this Republic in the north was aided by coincidences and happy developments, although nothing went the way the rebels ever wished it to go. The perseverance of the Calvinists, the inspiring leadership of William of Orange, the clever policy and strategy of the duumvirate Maurice-Oldenbarnevelt and the wealth of Holland kept the Republic on its feet and built it up into an European power of great significance.

# 12     **Prosperous Holland**

*15th - 18th century*

The Dutch Revolt would not have been successful in the last resort had not Holland, as the core of the resistance, been economically able to cope with the rising costs of defence and warfare. The wealth of the county of Holland carried the rebels to their victories. The foundations of Holland's prosperity had already been laid in the 14th and 15th century: the province was geographically situated in the centre of many European routes. Exchange of goods developed between north and south, east and west. Holland benefited from this traffic and busied itself with trans-shipment, storage and the carrying trade. Only a few products were supplied by Holland itself. In the first place: the herring. This fish, having had migrated from the Baltic area to the North Sea in the course of the 13th century, became an important trading object, mostly due to the invention of a suitable method of preservation: the so-called 'curing' (gutting and salting the fish immediately after the catch). The salt needed for this operation had to be carried from the south, from Portugal in particular. The curing of the herring, which had to be done on deck, stimulated the building of ships with wider decks and more space. Thus the 'kogge-boat' came into use in the 14th century, the 'fluyt' (fluteship) in the 16th. Many of the salt-carrying fishermen became merchant-sailors. Then there was beer, brewed in many Dutch towns since the 14th century. With the supply of grain, also needed for the increasing population in this waterridden country, trade relations with the Baltic developed. Weaving and selling of cloth became another early item of trade, centered in Leiden and Haarlem. And finally cattle-raising and the production of butter and cheese became intensive methods of using the rich soil of the Holland-polders.

A native shipping trade and ship-building industry, some exportable home products, a strong demand for several foreign products, and finally an extremely favourable geographical position were all-important factors in the creation of Holland's prosperity. In the Baltic trade the Dutch fleet, working at lower costs, crowded out the Hanseates. Building and equipping ships was helped by what was known as shared ownership. Small investments were put together to form a capital sufficient for getting a ship into commission. After each trip the profits on the freight were shared. Scant opportunities for other types of investment drew profits constantly back into trade and shipping. In particular Amsterdam, suitably situated in a bay of the Zuyder Zee (the IJ), enjoyed at that time the full advantages of this development: the sea-routes were avoided and inland water routes preferred. Special connections were established from Amsterdam with the corn-exporting port of Danzig. Other merchant cities, such as towns along the river IJssel and Dordrecht, clinging to traditional but inconvenient Hansa agreements on price and monopoly, were soon overshadowed by the young, new port of Amsterdam in the course of the 15th century. Other Zuyder Zee ports such as Enkhuizen and Hoorn did not have the same convenient inland water routes with the hinterland which Amsterdam could offer.

All this put Holland in a position to cope adequately with the important economic and political changes of the 16th century. With the discovery of the ocean route to the East Indies and the Americas trade shifted from the Mediterranean area to the west coast of Europe. The rapidly growing population all over Europe increased the demand for bulk products such as grain and timber, while the decline of the German and Baltic Hansa left the Dutch traders a free hand in the Baltic. Politically the Dutch Revolt caused important changes in economic affairs. Amsterdam's strongest competitor in international trade, Antwerp, fell into the hands of the Spanish in 1584. Many Flemish merchants left the town and settled in Amsterdam, bringing with them not just their transportable wealth but also their experience, their contacts and their special knowledge and technique of the trade to this city. The fact that Antwerp never recovered from this blow helped Amsterdam to consolidate its temporary advantage. Antwerp could not be reconquered by the Dutch rebels, but the northern troops settled down firmly north and south of the mouth of the Scheldt (Flushing and Sluis), which meant that a toll could be exacted on Antwerp's trade, or a blockade put into force. For two centuries Antwerp was to all extents cut off, to the advantage of Holland.

It was also as a result of the Revolt that Holland's shipping and trade began to venture outside the more traditional routes in Europe. The cause of war and trade could be served by attacking the Spanish-Portuguese colonial territories in America and Asia. Where the Spanish and Portuguese enemy (Portugal had been annexed by Spain in 1580) made such vast profits, the Dutch conquerors could do equally well. Ships from Holland and Zeeland swarmed out in all directions after 1590. Reckless enterprise and local military preponderance helped the Dutch to capture several Portuguese and even English settlements in the Indonesian Archipelago, in Malaya, India, Ceylon, and in Formosa and Japan. In 1602 a private trading company had been founded - the United East India Company - to which the government of the Dutch Republic granted the monopoly for trade and the right of diplomatic and military settlements in East Asia. The shareholders of the Company stayed at home, a relatively small group of Company administrators and soldiers were sent out to the widely distant and far-flung fortresses and trading-stations to watch over the interests of the Company. Most of these distant settlements of the Company were not very vast affairs: only the Moluccas, the eastern chain of islands of Indonesia, where native spice plantations of nutmeg and cloves were found, were soon taken over by Company agents who could thus monopolize the entire export of spices.

The centre for this vast network of Company settlements became the old Javanese town of Jacatra on the island of Java: there the fortress of Batavia was founded in 1619 (Djakarta today). The strong hand of Governor Jan Pietersz. Coen (1587 - 1629), conqueror of the Moluccas and founder of Batavia, had in fact created the more permanent and secure supremacy of the Company over an extensive area in the East-Asian world, based mainly on seapower and monopolization of ocean trade. It was only gradually, and in particular during the 18th century, that the main isles of this commercial empire, Java and Ceylon, were drawn into the sphere of Company power. In general the Company limited its interests mainly to the occupation of strategically and economically favourable stations in the coastal areas. Native rulers were forced into trade contracts and left to their own internal affairs as long as they did not clash with the commercial and contractual interests of the Company. In this way the native population was initially hardly touched by the influence of the Company - they noticed it only indirectly by an increased pressure from their own rulers who shifted the burden of their obligations towards the Company onto the population. Only those members of the population who lived on the coast or moved to the ports would notice that Arab and Chinese traders and skippers had been replaced by Dutch merchants and administrators, and that their native shipping organization was hindered by Dutch control. Not until the 19th century did contact between the Dutch and Indonesian native population become closer. The foundation of a halfway station on the Cape of South Africa by Jan van Riebeeck (1652) was of a different nature. On the long trip to Asia this station was intended to supply fresh vegetables and meat, and here, more than elsewhere, there grew a settlement of Dutch farmers, who, with reinforcements of French-Huguenot and German immigrants, penetrated into the hinterland to find better soil for extensive agriculture. In spite of the perhaps numerical superiority of the French and German elements in this Dutch Boer society and of British political supremacy after 1806, this growing 'people's plantation' preserved its own specific Dutch character. To this day the language (Afrikaans), spoken by a large part of the white population is closely related to Dutch, and the Calvinist religion is still very strong with these white 'Afrikaanders'.

A West Indian Company, provided with a special charter as was its East Indian counterpart, was founded in 1621 to conquer the Spanish-Portuguese colonies in the Americas. Here, however, the profits were less abundant or spectacular than in the Far East, except for the looting of Spanish Silver Fleets and the slave trade. In North America a colony of New Holland had been founded by settlers from Manhattan in 1614. By the time the English conquered it in 1667 it had spread into the surrounding country with about 10,000 mostly Dutch colonists. Its capital town, New Amsterdam, was to change its name to New York in later centuries. In the Caribbean area the island of Curaçao became a trading centre in 1634 and remained an important port for importing negro slaves from the west coast of Africa and exporting them to the mainland of South and Central America. In 1666, during a war with the English, a large territory, Surinam, on the north coast of South America was seized from them and this remained in Dutch hands. Further south the West Indian Company had settled in the Portuguese territory of Brazil (Olinda and Recife) in 1630, hoping to make of this important sugar-producing area a Dutch plantation in the heart of the Spanish empire, but the Portuguese put an end to these dreams thirty years later. The fortress of San George of Elmina on the Gold coast of Africa (nowadays Ghana) became for this company a temporarily vital export station for the slave trade.

However spectacular this expansion outside Europe might have been with all the consequences for the Netherlands in the centuries to come, the trade inside Europe during the 17th and 18th centuries remained of much greater importance to the prosperity of the Republic. Above all, the Baltic trade was still the mainstay of economic prosperity throughout this period. Only when bearing in mind that the Baltic trade was the 'mother-trade' of the Dutch Republic, can one understand the expansion of Dutch trade within Europe. New connections with Russia, Sweden, Italy and the Levantine coast were possible only by building upon the experience and the trading products which came from the traditional Baltic trade, and from the older contacts with French, English and Portuguese ports. The flourishing trade and shipping boosted the entire economic life of this young Republic. Amsterdam became the centre of gigantic money and banking business, including a lively trade in currency, drafts and shares. Here, Italian and Antwerp experiences in bookkeeping and banking techniques were of inestimable help. Manufacturing industry became an important link in the import and export business, for example the development of the Zaan area north of Amsterdam, where windmills had come into use from 1590 onwards on a large scale. These mills, of the most diverse types, for milling, grinding, sawing, hummed with activity. Carried to all the corners of the world by sail, some typical Dutch industrial products became internationally famous - Delft blue ware, diamonds from Amsterdam, beautiful books and atlases, prints and pamphlets, silverware from Schoonhoven, Dutch paper, cloth from Leiden and linen from Haarlem. Agriculture also prospered at a time of increasing trade. The extensive land reclamation projects - this time of some of the larger lakes - which intensified agriculture and horticulture, became feasible projects thanks to the abundance of capital. In due course many agricultural products also became famous - cheese and butter, vegetables and fruit, tulips and other flowers. The hub of this economic activity was centred in Amsterdam, and its influence was most strongly felt in the provinces of Holland, Zeeland and Friesland, the three 'sea-provinces'. From Amsterdam energy was channelled to other centres, before returning to this thriving city of picturesque semi-circular canals which grew far beyond its old medieval walls and was at this time 'the world's warehouse'.

*Page 78 Self-portrait of Rembrandt*

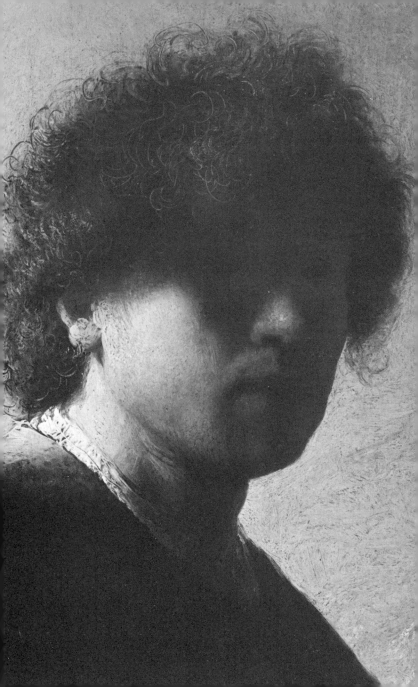

# 13     The 'Golden Age'

*17th century*

The range and depth of the cultural life of the young Republic in the 17th century was indeed a miracle: not only did the solid gold of prosperity glitter, but a living culture shone with dazzling brilliance, studded with outstanding names in every field of science, literature or arts. Such names come to mind as Hugo de Groot (1583 - 1645) scholar of international law, the physicist Christiaan Huygens (1629 - 1695), the inventor and user of the microscope Anthonie van Leeuwenhoek (1632 - 1723) and the great philosopher Baruch Spinoza (1632 - 1677), just to mention the most famous in scholarship. But there were many other glorious names of poets, composers, historians, architects. The fine arts, especially painting, rose to the greatest heights, with artists such as Rembrandt Harmensz van Rijn (1606 - 1669), Johannes Vermeer van Delft (d. 1675), Frans Hals (d. 1666), Jan Steen, Ruysdael, Van Goyen, Van Ostade, Van der Velde father and son, and many others. One hardly knows where to stop: words are incapable of describing the wealth and abundance of this vigorous unfolding of both arts and sciences, which can only be fully understood by detailed and specialized study.

All we can do here is point out some of the factors which may account for this abundance of culture.

Undoubtedly there was a relationship between economic prosperity and the high level of science and arts. Often these relationships were of an indirect nature, but sometimes there were also direct links. The progress of science and empirical research was aided by the practical needs of trade and shipping. Navigation required good charts and reliable astronomy, and the knowledge of foreign or even exotic languages. Political interference was supported by a thorough juridical knowledge of the theories on free navigation and free fishing. Grotius laid this down in his clever thesis 'Mare Liberum', later to be followed by his great work on international law 'De jure belli ac pacis'. The mathematician Simon Stevin worked out a better system of bookkeeping. Telescopes were improved and the refinement of lenses made possible microscopic research. The demand for financial efficiency in managing state credit by selling life insurances induced the scientist Huygens and the statesman De Witt to calculate and tabulate mortality rates.

The arts also flourished as a result of economic prosperity. More so than today they were functional, glorifying or gratifying the state and its rulers, ornamenting the town halls and the stately mansions.

Commissions were given for portraits, landscapes and still life to adorn the homes of rich burghers. Paintings were highly paid for and a proper trade developed with great export potential particularly for internationally popular landscapes. Rembrandt himself was a most successful and even wealthy painter, who only lost touch with his patrons at the end of his life. Vondel, the famous poet of his time, wrote verse on commission for 'weddings and other functions'. In architecture, the functional purpose was even more obvious. The beautiful decorations of old rebuilt towers by Hendrick de Keyzer, the stately mansions along the town canals by Vingboons and Marot, were perhaps outdone only by the regal grandeur of the huge town hall, built by Jacob van Campen on the Dam of Amsterdam. All the greatness of that greatest of cities was meant to be immortalized in this building by a collaboration of the then best known and most honoured architects, sculptors, painters and bell-founders, while the stadtholder whenever he visited the city had to make do with a residence in a highclass city tavern.

This functional character of many aspects of science and arts in the service of the leading citizens also largely explains the kind of realism that penetrated the culture of the Dutch golden age. Plain level-headed thinking helped science to continue, in some ways independent of the honoured authorities of Churches and Antiquity, directed rather towards practical experiment and experience. The Church, already split by the Reformation, did not succeed in recovering its earlier dominant position in science and culture, in spite of the fact that the Calvinist Church had become the only officially recognized one. Most of the rich citizens, the actual employers and patrons of those who were culturally creative, remained dogmatically indifferent and often tolerant in principle. Science even dared question the Bible as the only source of certainty and explanation of the wonders of the world. The great reverence for the classics helped on the one hand to push theological and biblical considerations aside and on the other to open up new sources of understanding and explanation. And even interpretation became less and less traditional, sometimes giving way to logical thought and reasoning apparently even exclusively. The great philosopher Descartes, who strongly influenced thought in the Netherlands, resided here for a long time. Spinoza boldly wrote against official church dogmas. Anatomical theatres became centres for medical scientific empirical research and demonstration. Microscopes and collections of curiosities, where strange objects such as exotic butterflies, skeletons and stuffed animals from faraway countries were on display, helped new research in natural history.

The same kind of sober realism was evident in the arts. A realistic view of life in its most practical aspect is clearly seen even in Hooft's prose and Vondel's verse, in spite of their classical and baroque framework. Realism often seemed to be the main feature in painting - in the brilliant space of Ruysdael's landscapes, in the breezy openness of Van de Velde's seas, in the serenity of an open oyster depicted by Kalff or in the buoyant portraits of Frans Hals.

Of course all this could be hidden again by allegory, edifying allusions, stylistic mannerisms, and it is also true to say that a great deal of technical skill and even tricky inventiveness could make Dutch paintings a source of entertainment and sophisticated discussion. But even here Dutch painting kept to its basic kind of realism, showing theatrically rather than dramatically, with inventiveness rather than deep analysis, instructive rather than deeply religious, what beauties and realities daily life and natural environment had to offer. It is in this that the slightly ironical genre-pieces by Jan Steen were more medial and typical of what the Dutch burghers appreciated than the remote 'difficult' paintings of Rembrandt in his later life. It is here that perhaps another factor should be mentioned explaining the kind of realism that was typical for Dutch 17th century cultural life. The rich citizen, although a patron or Maecenas for science and the arts, was not very far removed from the common people. He was after all a common man himself, a merchant or a skipper, a shopkeeper or a craftsman, and in his tastes and thoughts he came pretty close to what the ordinary Dutch man liked and disliked. He had had, of course, academic training, knew Latin and Roman law, and through his travels outside the Republic had met with sciences and arts very different from Dutch traditional art and science; but only gradually, in two or three generations, did this international and highclass cultural attitude begin to dominate his habits and thoughts: in the 18th century French became the 'chic' language. During the 17th century these regents and rich citizens seemed to be more bourgeois and simple in their behaviour and tastes, and their Protestant belief in thrift, singleness of heart and solidity helped them to appreciate forms of expression that could be considered to be useful, sound and edifying. Glorification and baroque expansiveness were aspects of a kind of monarchic absolutism they could only allow when such abstract ideas as the Republic, the City or the Family were to be honoured. For this reason not many great palaces were built in the 17th century in the Dutch Republic - Frederick Henry built his 'Huis ten Bosch' near the Hague and William III his palace near Apeldoorn (Het Loo), but that was about all - a few churches and many proud town halls were erected, but the main features of Dutch art were paintings, tapestries, clocks, books, meant to be on show inside the houses of the burghers. Intimacy and homeliness were more typical of Dutch art and Dutch science than expansive propaganda or exuberant conspicuousness.

Dutch 17th century civilization was characterized by another important factor - the political freedom of the Republic. Although there was one officially recognized Church, and although the one and only valid dogma accepted was that of Calvinism, rigidly outlined at the Synod of Dordrecht (1619), in practice the rich citizens turned away from the actual authority of the Church. Within that Church most of the middle and lower classes and a majority of the country people in most provinces gathered. Their leaders, ministers, however, were no match against the political and cultural superiority of the upper ruling classes. On the contrary, within the Church a certain spiritual impoverishment of this dogmatism seemed unavoidable, internal dissensions and narrowminded squabbles weakened it.

In everyday life the power of the citizens therefore brought about in practice freedom of religion, of the press and of assembly in most provinces and cities. The law did not permit that official posts should go to dissenters and certainly not to Roman Catholics, but both dissenters and Roman Catholics enjoyed a fair amount of freedom. They were allowed to build their churches, as long as they were not identifiable as such from the outside; they were allowed to organize their public services, as long as a small additional fee was paid; and they could organize their own care for the poor and sick of their communities. This freedom gave religious life a new spur and development, in particular in dissenting and sectarian Protestant groups. Mennonites, Remonstrants and Lutherans could develop their own special branches of Protestant dogma and morality. An individualistic mysticism could exist side by side with a warm community life within new sects like the 'Rijnsburger Collegianten'.

Practical freedom of the press made Amsterdam particularly an international centre of free speech and free print. Many a persecuted person from another country found a safe haven in the Dutch Republic. Foreign colonies were formed, such as those of Portuguese and of German-Polish Jews, who built their own synagogues and were free to live where they pleased (obligatory ghettos were unknown), and settled particularly within the walls of Amsterdam. The French Protestants, the Huguenots, who in absolutist France were exposed to increasing danger of losing their possessions and even their lives, found hospitality in the Republic, from 1680 onwards in particular. Most important was perhaps the influx from the Southern Netherlands of Flemish and French-speaking immigrants after the successful rebellion of the Northern Netherlands. This also meant a powerful reinforcement of Dutch culture, especially in the beginning of the 17th century. Many foreign scholars came to the Republic in their search for freedom: Descartes from France (1596 - 1650) published his major works here, the Czech Komensky (Comenius), a learned pedagogue (1592 - 1670), fled from intolerant Bohemia and Poland to die in Amsterdam and to be buried in Naarden. John Locke (1632 - 1704) lived in Holland during the 'eighties, when the English 'popish' kings made it impossible for him to remain in England. The Portuguese Jew Spinoza (1632 - 1677) could build up his philosophy in peace and freedom, although his own community had expelled him. And Pierre Bayle (1647 - 1706) started his great publishing activities after the sad and terrible experiences in hostile France had driven him to Rotterdam. Prosperity and freedom, and a kind of realistic soberminded bourgeois mentality formed fertile soil for a flourishing culture. But those factors do not explain why in this Dutch sky such miraculously blinding comets could appear - sources of constant wonder to the entire world. Their own gifts raised them far above all others - Rembrandt, Huygens, Grotius and Spinoza. To explain this greatness is impossible.

# 14    The formation of the frontiers

*17th century*

In the course of the 17th century the Dutch Republic
became a more definite unity with a stronger inner
cohesion. The frontiers for the territory as a whole were
more sharply drawn than ever before and within these
frontiers there grew up something akin to patriotic feeling,
strongly influenced by the provincial preponderance of
Holland.
In the west and north everything had been clearly outlined
since the beginning of history: here the Dutch Republic was
bordered by the natural frontier of the sea. The various
wars between the Republic and England (1652 - 1654,
1665 - 1667, 1672 - 1674) could have no influence on these
natural borders. In these wars trade interests across the
oceans and in the distant overseas settlements were at
stake, not the territory on the continent, although
sometimes Charles II thought of getting a foothold on the
Zeeland isles or acquiring nominal sovereignty over the
Republic. The coastline of the North Sea demarcated the
shape of the Dutch Republic without any fear of change.
The eastern boundary was much harder to define. A couple
of rivers and swamps did in some way help to indicate an

# The frontiers of the low-countries

*about 1300*

*charles V (1548)*

*1648*

*1839 (with actual coastline)*

outline, but they certainly did not form 'natural borders'. Relations with the east were even more complicated because formally the Republic still belonged, as had been the case in the Middle Ages, to the Holy Roman Empire of the Germans, and the elected Emperor remained the highest liege lord of most of the territories which formed the Republic. On paper these bonds continued to exist, but in practice they had weakened in the 16th century and had been broken in the 17th century. After 1728 the German Emperor, a Habsburg in Vienna, who had until then maintained the fiction of his high feudal rights, appears finally to have dropped his claims in the Northern Netherlands.

In any case, these formal feudal ties bore no real relation to the actual development of the frontier. Many areas which gradually came to belong to Germany were in the 17th century strongly influenced by the Republic. Several small towns and regions were militarily occupied by Dutch troops for quite long periods, such as East Frisia, Bentheim, Cleve, Emmerich and Rees. The Republic later abandoned these areas out of sheer indifference. These regions were agriculturally poor, and the political and economic weakness of Germany during the 16th and 17th centuries left a vacuum along the Dutch eastern frontiers which was only filled by the Republic if military and strategical interests required it. The Republic more often neglected than cared for its interests in the east: attention was mainly directed towards the west and the south. The Republic's neglect of its eastern borders, however, led to attacks by the bishops of Münster and Cologne, bribed with English and French money, which created unnecessary dangers in 1666 and 1672, and this neglect meant that the actual formal situation was as it had been left by the former rulers Charles V and Philip II. The somewhat winding border was the result of tradition, dynastic feudal regulations and pure coincidence rather than of strategic and political calculation. But gradually these border areas developed and the inhabitants on both sides acquired a feeling of cultural and even national difference. Technically the eastern provinces of the Dutch Republic became part and parcel of a Dutch system of administration and trade. The great prosperity of the province of Holland drew these eastern provinces economically and culturally towards it, and the lower German dialects which were often the language used by the people on both sides of the border, gradually vanished in the areas which belonged to the provinces of Gelderland (the so-called Achterhoek), Overijssel (Twente) and the eastern parts of Drente and Groningen. A kind of Dutch that was generally understood, helped by the official language used and strongly influenced by Hollandisms, replaced Lower German. Protestantization, moreover, largely since Maurice's conquest in 1590s, helped in this process. The ministers from Holland and the new Dutch translation of the Bible and the psalms not only led people to the new religion, but also smoothed away the differences between the west and the east within the Dutch Republic. It may be true that in some of the most eastern areas Counter Reformation had already done its work before the Dutch rebels settled and some areas like Twente and Achterhoek remained Roman Catholic. But even this did not stop the increasing influence of Holland after the successful Dutch revolt.

In the German areas on the other side of this frontier a reverse process took place at a much slower rate. Most frontier areas came under the supreme power of Brandenburg (later the Kingdom of Prussia) and the official High German language took the place of the Lower German dialects, and in the course of the 18th century a real frontier became established where previously an area of gradual transition had existed.

The formation of the southern frontier took a much more arbitrary and unsteady course. When in 1621 the war against Spain was taken up again - the revolutionary spirit having entirely faded - sorties took place across the large rivers into the provinces of the Spanish Netherlands. Stadtholder Maurice and his brother Frederick Henry tried in this way to shift the battleground into enemy country in the hope that discontent and unrest in these areas would possibly bring back a situation in which many provinces in the south would again join the fight on the side of the northern 'rebels'. But again and again these assaults only resulted in some slight territorial gain. Frederick Henry made a spectacular conquest of 's-Hertogenbosch after a long, technically perfect siege in 1629. When the same stadtholder ventured further south with a sally deep in enemy territory, he got stuck in conquered Maastricht (1632). The Peace of Münster which put an end to this long-drawn-out war did not do much more than confirm these accidental conquests (1648) - the Barony of Breda, the Bailiwick of 's-Hertogenbosch and the enclave of Maastricht remained in the possession of the Republic. The treatment meted out to these conquered lands was in sharp contrast to that of the earlier liberated territories. The religious differences, which could no longer be overcome by a rapid protestantization, nullified every attempt at co-operation on a basis of equality. These 'popish' territories were no more than appendices of the sovereign protestant provinces. The fact that Roman Catholic church ceremonies were officially and for a long time practically forbidden was another unfortunate consequence of these conquests. The Counter Reformation had successfully brought most of the population back into the fold of traditional worship and sacraments before the northern Dutch troops were able to enter these areas, and this population which stuck to its traditional Church suffered from discrimination as a consequence. Not until well into the 18th century were these poor and rural districts south of the great rivers allowed to make the slightest progress.

South of this border lived Flemish and French-speaking populations under the rule of Spanish governors. A certain feeling of affinity in race and language between these inhabitants and those in the Dutch Republic continued to exist in an increasingly subdued way. Trade interests in Holland and Zeeland and political fear of French imperialism furthered mutual estrangement of those who had before the Dutch Revolt belonged to the same collective structure of states under their 'natural ruler'. The right to levy almost prohibitive taxes on ships coming from Antwerp and passing the Scheldt estuaries was underlined by the Peace Treaty of 1648, and this was to remain Flanders' never-ending grudge against the north. The fear of French aggression, which had become increasingly ominous since Louis XIV (1661), tempted the Republic to use the south as a buffer state against possible French attacks. That again and again, the Southern Netherlands had thus to submit to being a battlefield seemed unimportant.

Nevertheless, in the end this policy dit not prove profitable enough for the Republic. In 1672 French troops, in a wide encircling movement through western German lands, crossed the IJssel. Only the water line near Utrecht saved Holland and only the tough defence led by stadtholder William III (1672 - 1702) at last succeeded in repulsing the French troops by an equally widesweeping operation towards the eastern borders of the Republic where the French troops were threatened to be cut off. The same stadtholder later used his position as stadtholder in the Republic and as King of England (1688) in the struggle against French hegemony and expansion. After three wars, French power was finally kept within bounds (1672 - 1678, 1688 - 1697 and 1701 - 1713). It is no exaggeration to say that the Republic spent itself militarily and politically in these endless and costly wars. The new regulations for the southern frontier after 1715 were therefore nothing but torture for the Southern Netherlands and merely a shallow display of power for the north. Troops recruited and paid by the Dutch Republic were stationed at Namur, Doornik, Ypres and Dendermonde to form a military 'barrier' against France. This arrangement caused nothing but ill-feeling among the Flemish who had to pay for this 'barrier' but at the same time saw how under their very eyes these fortresses were neglected and fell into disrepair. In 1745 - 1746, when the Republic was once again drawn into an international conflict, the barrier was easily overrun by French troops. A hasty but, miraculously, not unfavourable peace saved the Republic in 1748. In 1781 the barrier was finally dispensed with when the ruler of the Southern Netherlands, the Austrian Emperor Joseph II, demanded and obtained an immediate evacuation. There was not much the Republic could have done at that stage: a desperate war with England required all its attention and the occupying troops in the Flemish cities were practically helpless in dilapidated fortifications and without any good training for defence. The utter senselessness of this barrier lends an even more tragic colouring to the estrangement between north and south.

*17th century*

The Dutch Revolt had not created a new, well-organized state overnight. The entire rebellion had been directed against the central government of Brussels. When this central power fell, tendencies to disintegration grew. Each district, each city made a big issue of its rights and privileges and was only interested in the largest possible autonomy for itself. Stadtholders, even William of Orange, were only tolerated because they were needed in the common struggle against the enemy, and only were they allowed strong military power. The relations between the provinces had been more or less accidentally settled in the Union of Utrecht (1579) which originated as a defensive agreement against Parma's advance, and the various regions and cities never attempted a better or more precise arrangement than this. Even after the loss of some of the signatories such as Flanders and the cities of Brabant, the old agreement was kept alive as an honoured and hallowed basis of loose co-operation. The Republic of the United Provinces would never be more than a federation.
Even within each of the seven equal provinces of the federation the situation was complicated by many smaller

units of autonomy and power. In Holland for instance Amsterdam had a paramount position and often took the lead within the county of Holland, sometimes against the wishes and views of the other cities and magistrates in the province. The IJssel cities in Overijssel, the well-to-do farmers in Friesland, the nobility and gentry in Gelderland had their special position of influence within the structure of government of each province, legally and in practice. The provinces of Friesland, Groningen and Drente had another separate stadtholder, a descendant of William of Orange's brother from the 'Frisian' Nassau line. The federation itself was governed by an assembly of provincial delegations (the States General), which only by seven unanimous votes could take decisions on common federal issues such as foreign affairs, religion and defence. The deputies within the delegations were bound to the instructions they had received from their commissioners, the provincial estates, and if decisions had to be taken which differed from these instructions, new orders had to be awaited from the provincial capitals. And since within these provincial estates the deputies representing the cities or the nobility could be at odds, decision-making was often very slow and sometimes almost impossible.

One may wonder how so much was achieved in spite of this complicated and unsatisfactory institutional structure. Human inventiveness and adaptability, competent statemanship, personal influence and internal class solidarity oiled this rather creaking and rusty machine. More important, however, were the two major powers which, usually in turn, sometimes in co-operation, held things together and kept things going - the Grand Pensionary and the Stadtholder. In the government of the province of Holland the Grand Pensionary was the highest official, and thanks to the superior wealth and power of this province, he had extensive influence in the Union. Paradoxically Holland strongly supported the federal government, but it meant in practice that Holland could rule the Republic to a great extent in a complicated semi-centralized way. Holland supplied more than half the state finances, and consequently the vote of this province had more weight than the other six together. Thus the Grand Pensionary, official leader of the Holland delegation in the States General, could take charge of Union affairs - he called the meeting of the States General, he drew up the agenda, he drafted decrees and wrote letters to the Dutch ambassadors and envoys abroad. The Grand Pensionary was, in fact, while formally remaining an employee of Holland, the 'Speaker' of the States General, the Minister of Foreign Affairs and the Head of the offices of the Union in one person. The most famous of these officials were Johan van Oldenbarnevelt (1586 - 1618: then still entitled 'Landsadvocaat'), Johan de Witt (1653 - 1672) and Anthony Heinsius (1689 - 1720). Statesmanlike in foreign politics, clever in home affairs, they competently steered the Republic between the dangerous rocks of international politics and risky wars for more than a century.

This display of Holland's preponderance and power was in facts borne by the rich regents, the rulers of the cities, and was often led by the - largest - city of Amsterdam. From their seats of local and regional power they could support or undermine the policies of the Union. Their solid financing helped the Union through most dangerous situations. Thanks to Holland a powerful fleet could be built and launched during the period 1650 - 1674. Indeed it was an awe-inspiring navy, not only because of its equipment, construction and speed, but also by reason of its efficiency, as was proved in encounters with the strong English fleet. In many naval wars and expeditions it gave an impressively successful performance. The famous admiral Michiel Adriaenszoon De Ruyter (killed in action in 1676) was perhaps the embodiment of the quiet and loyal courage of Holland's power and direction of affairs which, even in wartime, could be shown. There have also been periods when Holland could closely co-operate with the other interests and powers within the Republic. The valuable teamwork of Van Oldenbarnevelt and Prince Maurice (1586 - 1609) has been mentioned before. When, in 1672, the year of disaster for the Republic, both France and England pounced on it and De Witt was forced to resign, the new stadtholder William III could only resist the attack of the French with the brave and loyal help of the Amsterdam regents.

On the other hand, Holland's preponderance and leadership had its setbacks. Economic and political self-interest often took priority, and one of the disastrous consequences was neglect of the territorial defences and the army. Amsterdam's traditional rivalry against Antwerp prevented the Spanish Netherlands after 1648 from being the loyal allies the Republic would have needed. Internal squabbles within Holland or within several cities could create a vacuum of power which affected the union as a whole. In many ways, moreover, the rule of Holland was of course class-restricted and class-conscious in its effects and attitudes, excluding or estranging the loyalty of other groups and classes within the union, province or city. The 'lower' groups of craftsmen, shopkeepers and labourers were treated in a paternalistic way, often charitable but condescending and self-centred. The tax policy of these regents was a typical example of narrowmindedness: taxes were levied on foodstuffs for immediate use (excise on beer, flour, bread, cheese, etc.) while trade and property were exempt as far as possible. Soon taxation proved to be one of the heaviest burdens the general population had to carry.

It is understandable that for these reasons there existed opposition and even strife against the rule of the Holland regents within that province and even outside it. Such opposition tended to concentrate around the court of the family of the stadtholders. Although princes and counts by descent and title, the members of the Houses of Orange-Nassau and Nassau-Dietz (in Friesland) were nothing but officials within the seven provinces of the Union. But for a large section of the population these princely dynasties had a great tradition derived from William of Orange, who had been the leader of the Dutch Revolt, and his sons and great-grandson who gained glories on the battlefield. Though without definite plans for institutional reform or realistic centralization, the stadtholders were often the focus for support when discontent or local trouble came to a head. All those who opposed the Holland regents took the side of the stadtholders: the other provinces, worried about the neglect of their territorial and rural interests and the weakening of the army; the army officers, often recruited from the local nobility of Gelderland, Utrecht and Overijssel; and large sections of the middle and lower classes. Much of this discontent found an echo also within the official Calvinist (reformed) Church. Sometimes the Protestant clergy became the spokesmen of the socially destitute and discontented, and there grew a special link between the Calvinist Church and the stadtholders because William of Orange had made the Reformation possible and his House had been firmly Protestant ever since.

Clashes between the regents and the stadtholders with their mixed bag of supporters were sometimes unavoidable. As early as the time of the armistice with Spain (1609 - 1621) a dispute inside the Church developed into a severe struggle for power in which Prince Maurice defeated Van Oldenbarnevelt: the beheading of this grand old servant of the Republic put a temporary, abrupt and deeply tragic end to this struggle (1619). Later on stadtholders, inspired by French and English examples of absolutism and relying on the help of dissatisfied elements in the Republic, thought they could improve their own position by expanding their power. The younger son of William of Orange, Frederick Henry (stadtholder 1625 - 1647), gave himself princely airs, which the regents could hardly tolerate: he built a stately, though small, palace near The Hague, formed a real court of his own, gave his only son William in marriage to a daughter of the royal English Stuart line (1641). But it was only when this William succeeded his father as stadtholder (1647) that real trouble came. William II believed he could break Holland's opposition by a surprise attack on Amsterdam in 1650, but his premature death put a stop to the conflict (1651).

The regents took advantage of the situation by dispensing with the office of stadtholder and thanks to Johan de Witt's powerful leadership this government was maintained until 1672 - in spite of the fact that William II's son had become of age. However, when Holland's foreign policy collapsed and the Republic found itself suddenly confronted with the French and English enemies in alliance, de Witt was forced to resign and William III was appointed Stadtholder in 1672. The lynching of de Witt in The Hague in the same year showed the pitch to which the dissension had risen. William III, although taken by surprise himself, seized this opportunity to intimidate the regents by threatening to turn the anger of the populace against them. He succeeded in drawing a great deal of power into his own hands, and although he eventually proved less powerful than the regents had feared - he was chiefly interested in fighting the French and left the affairs to the regents more than he intended to do - after his death in 1702 the Holland regents hastily decided to leave the office of stadtholder vacant once again, in spite of the presence of the Frisian Nassau who had hoped to be made Stadtholder for all provinces of the Republic.

It would be unfair to hold the regents of Holland responsible for the many tensions in the 17th-century Republic. Certainly self-interest and narrow local patriotism were typical of their mentality, but on the other hand the stadtholders often served the interests of their dynasty before those of the Republic. The bonds with the Stuarts, strengthened once again in 1678 by William III's marriage to his cousin, daughter of James II of England, gave a foreign tinge to the House of Orange-Nassau. Many of the followers of the stadtholders were more negatively inspired by their opposition to Holland's supremacy and the arrogance of the regents, than positively drawn by loyalty to the dynasty of the stadtholders' family or towards any decisive state reform. If the stadtholders had really acquired kingly power, where but with the very regents they fought against would they have found solid support and reasonable security? The high-class burghers were the only people mature enough to take part in matters of government and they certainly would not have acquiesced easily to a system of royal absolutism with its bad consequences for the interests of prosperity and peace. In fact, the basic reality of the power of the Dutch Republic still rested with those regents who were the best people in the right position to decide the fate of the provinces.

# 16     Slow decline

*18th century*

It was the aristocracy of the regents and especially of those of the province of Holland that kept the Dutch Republic afloat. Even the more powerful authority of Stadtholder William III, if he had fully used it, would not have changed this situation. But during the course of the 18th century it looked as if these regents were slackening their hold. It would be unfair to explain this by taking a look at the sometimes arrogant faces under powdered wigs which we see in many a portrait of an 18th century Dutch aristocratic regent. There may have been much smug contentment and degenerate luxury: accusations of corruption, nepotism and abuse of power became more frequent, coming to a head at times of crisis. But it is doubtful whether basically the regents of the 18th century were any worse than their forbears. What we now call corruption, was accepted as the legitimate spoils of power at that time, but it may be true that these wealthy rulers, who by habit and inheritance succeeded their fathers and grandfathers in the seats of power, took things too much for granted and, neglecting to make use of their abilities and qualifications, sometimes let things slide.

But more important perhaps than this explanation of a certain smugness and lack of energy may be the fact that the regent class began to isolate itself socially from the lower classes of society. The seats of power became by tradition the privilege of certain high-ranking families in each city and each province. Descent, marriage, personal relations began to matter more than ability and quality. Had it been only a matter of choice, of course, those who were most able or at least most skilful or adaptable within these circles would succeed to positions of power in the end, and often individual regents proved their worth in a highly satisfactory way. But such choices were limited by the growing exclusiveness of the group and the lower strata of society could no longer replenish and support it as it had done before. This exclusiveness was not just a matter of internal regulations by which the best official positions were handed down only to relative and friends, but also of cultural exclusiveness in the use of the French language, in the strict rules of manners and habits and a refined fashionableness. The Dutch 'élite' formed only a thin upper layer which, by losing touch with the common people, started to crack. As happens when tiny cracks appear in the surface of an old painting, it will remain a good picture for a long time: at a distance the cracks do not bother the spectator, but on close inspection they show the beginnings of decay.

In the development of culture this exclusiveness of the 'élite' stifled stylized manifestations of art. Foreign influences were welcomed, and in literature classical forms were the pattern for a rather artificial kind of verse and prose. Bredero's sincere and human farces of the first half of the 17th century were elbowed out by Pieter Langendijk's (1683 - 1756) imitations of Molière. In the pictorial arts the intimate and realistic interpretations gave way to portraits - certainly no less clever - of fashionable importance and to baroque landscapes in the French and Italian style. Soon Rococo made its appearance and furniture and tapestry imitated Boucher and Fragonard. All this did not exclude a certain homely humour and intimacy, but it certainly never reached the artistic heights the 17th century had known. Even in the field of science, inventiveness and originality dwindled. Herman

Boerhaave's name (1668 - 1738) would still be recognized around the world as that of a great physician, who by his work and publications brought together all the knowledge and experience medicine had collected in the course of his times, but he was a great compiler and an excellent systematic teacher rather than an original inventive scientist.

Though unfortunate, it was not just coincidental, that during the 18th century the Republic met with unfavourable political and economic situations. From the political point of view it had lived above its station - its gradual loss of political influence was therefore to be expected though certainly not easy to understand at the time, nor easy to accept by those who thought of the Dutch Republic as a great European power. In the 17th century it had been able to play the role of a European power solely due to a situation of strife between England and France which maintained the balance while the power of the Habsburgs had declined. While avoiding a collision with these powers, the Republic's main pursuit had been the peaceful development of its own shipping and trade. It had not aggressively strived for prestige or enlargement of continental territory, at most it carried on an aggressive trade policy in the Baltic and the Asiatic and American areas. However, when France ventured into wars of expansion outside her frontiers and when England increased her power as a commercial rival on the seas, the Republic's political supremacy began to weaken. The Republic had had its share in the coalitions against France, organized by William III. After his death (1702), Heinsius had continued this policy to the bitter end of a difficult peace (1713), and the Republic was exhausted. The alliance with England - strengthened in the person of William III who had obtained the English and Scottish thrones in 1688 - meant that in due course the Republic had to follow in the wake of England, and under this safeguard the army and even the navy were neglected. Only because of its tradition of great power and the self-assuredness with which the regents kept up appearances did the Republic manage to keep its place on the stage of the 18th century international politics for a long time. Even in two wars in which it became involved against its wish, the Republic pulled through fairly well. The first war stopped just in time in 1748 as a result of English support, before the French could try to cross the rivers. In the second war (1780 - 1784), which was hopelessly unsuccessful for the Dutch, the day was saved against the English by means of French aid.

In the 17th century the economic strength of the Republic had been based on shipping and trade, and this basis was inevitably vulnerable. As soon as other countries started to build up their own shipping and industry, the Dutch merchant navy had to suffer the consequences. Already in the second half of the 17th century, France and England introduced protectionist measures which aimed at excluding Dutch skippers and merchants from trading and shipping to those countries. Technical improvements in shipbuilding and more regular organized shipping traffic made the Dutch harbours as intermediate stations less necessary, and thus Holland lost part of her position as an entrepot station on which manufacturing industries particularly were dependent. As a result there was a decline in industry with unemployment in several of its sectors.

On the other hand, economic decline was slow and not easy to detect immediately. Trade and shipping were still busy enough. Dutch merchants kept things going by participating in world trade outside their own ports: they sent letters and instructions to their agents in far-away countries and to their skippers in foreign ports. The number of ships under sail and the turnover of goods did not show a dramatic decline, but it was clear that England outvied her Dutch rival and that the Republic had reached a point beyond which it could not go. The equipment of the ships became obsolete, and ships were used for a longer time than was advisable. But nevertheless in this same century the Amsterdam exchange remained a flourishing centre of finance and even expanded its international influence. Enough money had been made or was still being made to finance international loans and other such business. Equally spectacular were the successes of the East India Company, in spite of its many financial difficulties. During the 18th century, the great territorial expansion in South East Asia took place which finally turned this company into an institution of government and administration rather than an organization for trade only. Larger and larger parts of the large islands of Java and Ceylon were occupied by company troops or subjected to company authority. Internal dynastic wars invited interference in these hinterlands; new initiative in organizing plantations in some areas brought Dutch settlers further from the coast than ever before.

The rate of decline was therefore slow and contemporaries only recognized it as such very late in the day. The Republic continued to act as a major power in international politics, and for a long time enjoyed prosperity in trade and international finance. When at last the true situation was realized, the reaction was one of resignation rather than of renewed energy. More than anything the slowness of the process suggested fatal inevitability: if one looked for scapegoats, one could point to the stadtholders who, alas, proved to be uncommonly badly suited to their tasks. If one looked for the withholding of God's grace, one could point to the plague which played havoc among cattle, or to the rising sandbanks in front of the Amsterdam Zuyder Zee port, or to the dangerous pile-worm that ruined the wood in some dyke construction and caused floods. But to find the scapegoats or to prove God's disfavour did not help the situation: the pile-worm of defeat had already ruined the Republic internally before it started to bore away at the surface of dykes.

# 17     **Political revival**

*1747 - 1798*

The political and military weakness was brought into broad daylight for the first time in 1747, when the Republic was involved on the side of England in a war against France. French troops conquered Bergen-op-Zoom in a surprise attack and the regents dared neither continue nor stop the war for fear of an internal uprising, but such an uprising was soon a fact: the Frisian Stadtholder, descendant of the Nassaus, heir also to the titles of Orange, was recalled into the vacant stadtholderships of the western provinces. Thus the second period in which Holland and other provinces had dispensed with a stadtholder (1702 - 1747) had come to a sad end. The new Stadtholder, William IV, clearly knew what he wanted in the way of titles and position, less clearly perhaps did he see how to raise the Republic from its misery. In titles and authority he got what he wanted: a hereditary stadtholdership over all provinces and extended prerogatives in the appointment of government bodies. But he could not give much substance to all his titles and authority. Peace with France was possible not by a victory of the weak stadtholder's troops but thanks to a sudden change of the warlike mood of the English ally (1748). And his plans for a long overdue reform of government, a reorganization of navy and army, a recuperation of prosperity, were all strangled in red tape. The expectations of many, that William IV would break the supreme power of the regents by giving the middle classes, who were excluded from political influence, some kind of say in the administration, were not fulfilled. Shocked rather than inspired by the violent uprising in 1747 and 1748 with their many undertones of economic and social discontent, William IV leaned more and more on the regents, who refused to be dislodged from their seats of power. He only grudgingly made some tax concessions under pressure of revolt and plundering, and that was all. The windows of the stadtholder's palace were hastily shut, preventing the escape of the stuffy atmosphere of governmental smugness.

For too long the people had believed that the cure for all ills was to be found in a firm stadtholdership. Disappointment in the stadtholder turned these feelings and expectations against him. Only *without* a stadtholder, it was felt, could something be done to improve matters. And it seems as if this new negative thought cleared the way for more positive thinking of a radical kind. French and particularly English enlightened ideas on what the ideal state should be and what part all free citizens should play within it, helped. Joan Derk van der Capellen (1741 - 1784) became the spiritual leader of a new radical movement of so-called Patriots. First he translated two books from the English before he himself set out a kind of program in an important pamphlet addressed 'To The People of the Netherlands' (1781). Old ideas about the freedom of the Teutons, about the medieval democracy of the guilds and on the Right of Insurrection, such as had served as a basis for the actual foundation of the Republic when Philip II was abjured, blended with the English and French ideas of thinkers like Price, Montesquieu and Rousseau. Based on the principle that authority was with the people as a whole (people's sovereignty) and that it was held in trust only by certain office-holders until their dismissal, demands were formulated to have the stadtholder's power and the regents' authority curbed, because they abused the people's confidence. Van der Capellen suggested the formation of minor political groups, to be trained and armed in cities and villages, so that pressure would be brought to bear on the administration of cities and provinces to reform the state.

Cultural life also seemed to revive with this political activity. Many societies and institutions were set up to find ways and means towards the improvement of society, morally, economically, socially and scientifically. Everything was viewed in a rational and technical spirit with a strong moralizing and socially sensitive purpose. Education and a new kind of educational welfare work seemed to be a panacea for many ills. Reports and enquiries about industrial and economic problems, pamphlets and tracts on morals and edification appeared with a rather more ethical than religious slant. Women authors such as Betje Wolff (1721 - 1790) and her friend Aagje Deken, influenced by the English novelist Richardson, tried to propagate in letters within the structure of a novel their message on what they considered to be useful, just and edifying.

In the 'eighties the first chances to give the Patriots real political influence presented themselves. For a long time it had been obvious that William's successor after his early death (1751), William V, would not achieve much. However, as long as no real trouble upset the state, the Orangists could hold on. The insurrection of the American colonies against England had the full attention of the Dutch public because of its bearing on trade and its political implications. France, engaged in war with England since 1778, lent diplomatic force to this sympathy for the American rebels, against which the traditional friends of England like the Stadtholder dared do nothing. Thus the Republic was dragged into a war with England (1780), and the extremely unfavourable course of this war was once again blamed on the Stadtholder who had failed as supreme commander of the army and the navy. The traditionally anti-stadtholder regents joined forces with the Patriots and tried even after the peace with England (1785) to undermine the position of the Stadtholder with the help of French diplomacy. In the following years the tension between Orangists and Patriots rose to such a pitch that civil war seemed inevitable. The Stadtholder left the province of Holland to organize his resistance in the other more loyal provinces and only by the grace of his clever spouse, Wilhelmina of Prussia, did William V return in 1787, backed by an expedition of Prussian troops and once more in the wake of English protection and overwhelm.

Yet not all was lost for this radical new political movement. The French revolution, started in 1789, turned the tide for the Dutch Republic six years later. When in 1795 - the Patriots had bided their time waiting and hoping - the French troops marched into the Northern Netherlands, they sparked off the Dutch revolution. The Stadtholder and his family fled to England: the French liberators were enthusiastically welcomed, delirious crowds danced around the trees of liberty (similar to maypoles in appearance). And indeed the old Republic of the United Provinces was reformed. During the first period in which the Patriots seemed to have had their chance (1785 - 1787), they only intended the curbing of the power of the Stadtholder and the regents within the framework of the old institutions, but now the past was radically put aside. A new Republic named after the old 'free' Teutonic tribe, the Batavian Republic, was created, and a National Assembly replaced the States General (1796), elected by universal male suffrage. All discrimination against poor regions and dissenting minorities was done away with: the provinces of Drente and Brabant had the same rights as the other provinces. Religious groups which had been discriminated against, such as the dissenters (Remonstrants, Lutherans, Mennonites etc.), the Roman Catholics and even the Jews were put on the same level as regards rights of citizenship with the Calvinists. Preparations were made for a full constitution accepted by the people - something previously unknown in the history of the Netherlands.

However, it soon appeared that the tide of revolutionary enthusiasm was receding. After endless discussions in the Assembly a draft constitution was put before the electorate which pleased nobody and was rejected. The behaviour of France, erstwhile ally and liberator, was a sad disappointment. Peace with its severe demands, which had been thrust down the Republic's throat, had been hard to digest, and the intrigues of French envoys created suspicion and unrest. The war which the new Republic had to fight with France against England meant the loss of practically all overseas settlements and territories and a large part of trade and shipping.

Internal division, moreover, weakened from the very beginning the force of political revival. Rich anti-stadtholder burghers had sided with the Patriots for their own political interests and convictions rather than inspired by really radical enlightened ideas. Where real change was at stake, the majority of these 'aristocrats', often still occupying the seats of power, remained passive and uninterested or even hostile. In Utrecht clashes had already occurred in 1785 between regent-Patriots and true democrats. The same divisions were to be found in the National Assembly after 1795. This time the fundamental bone of contention related to the structure of the state - was a real centralization desirable? - and to the actual democratic rights of all citizens - should they have the influence in government that some radicals proposed? The so-called 'federalists' were soon supported by all those who hoped for the return of the status quo, including the Orangists. After all, the revolution of 1795 had been a mild one leaving everybody in their positions, as long as they had not been too outspokenly Orangist, and it deserved the name of 'velvet revolution'. Against this growing opposition the Unitarians, the more radical Patriots, were no match: their chariot got stuck in the sands of opposition and traditionalism.

Discussions between these moderates and conservatives on the one hand and radicals and democrats on the other, went on for a long time, but the French could not wait. They were up to their necks in a war with England, and the Republic was too vital a stronghold to permit any dissension. Two coups d'état put an abrupt end to the endless discussions: the French envoy was deeply involved in both. French supremacy became more oppressive than ever and only in this way did a Patriot minority succeed in promulgating a first constitution of a rather radical sort (1798).

# 18      French domination

*1798 - 1813*

From 1798, politics in the Netherlands followed like a seismograph the political upheavals in France. The first coup d'état produced a unitarian administration, because the left-wing parties in France had more influence at that moment; the second coup followed a shift to the right in French politics. The structure of political institutions was also inspired by French examples: when a 'Directoire' of five members was set up in France, the Constitution of 1798 of the Batavian Republic instituted a similar administration. In 1799 Napoleon was raised to the position of first Consul: the Batavian Constitution of 1801 placed more power in the hands of a small executive. When Napoleon finally crowned himself Emperor in 1804, the Batavian Republic first had, in 1805, a Grand Pensionary with royal power, and then one of Napoleon's brothers, Louis Napoleon, as King over the 'Kingdom of Holland' (1806). With this last constitutional change the Batavian Republic, so proudly founded, went finally to its grave.
French authority pressed even harder on the Netherlands. It was of vital interest to them to continue the war, and the weakness of the Dutch defences were once again

demonstrated in 1799 when an invasion of North Holland by English and Russian troops took place. The last remnants of the old Dutch navy, traditionally Orangist, defected without resistance to the English fleet. The Batavian troops were unable to resist and the danger of an Orangist rising did not seem far off. Only powerful intervention by French troops saved the day, and with Napoleon's rise to power the pressure of the French, especially in strategic and defensive aspects, increased. Louis Napoleon, however, did not like to obey his brother and tried to become popular in his own kingdom by defending Holland's interests against the French. When finally a second English invasion, this time in 1809 in Zeeland, once again severely tested the Dutch defences, Napoleon decided to annex the kingdom to France in 1810.

We must be careful not to overrate this period as one only of wretchedness caused by foreign occupation. The annexation of the Netherlands by France in 1810 was a late and final stage in a progress which had left some leeway for the Dutch themselves to put in hand internal reforms and restricted constitutional improvements. National apathy changed to bitterness and hatred against the French only when, at the end of the period of annexation, the influence of the French empire in Europe began to wane. The arrival of the French troops in 1795 was really welcomed as a liberation by many Dutchmen: the great military successes of Napoleon had made a deep impression. Admiration for much that the French did, helped many over the feelings of disappointment and disillusion about the way the French treated the Dutch. This administration was not limited to the enlightened ideas which were formulated before and during the French revolution and mainly carried out by Napoleon, but was also stimulated by the organizational and administrative achievements in France which served as examples of what could be done locally. Failures of the independent and democratic Republic were often blamed on its own weakness and lack of unity rather than on French interference. It would be wrong to assign modern interpretations of 'treason' and 'collaboration' to this period. 'Collaboration' as such with the French was the 'crime' of all who stayed in the Netherlands instead of leaving with the exiled Stadtholder, and even some of these emigrants returned to the Republic after some years. After all the Stadtholder himself, on English advice, had not hesitated to 'call in' Prussian help, when he thought he needed it in his country (1787).

While the Batavian Republic failed in the realization of democratic and radical ideas, it succeeded in the end in putting many of these ideas into practice through reforms of government and administration. It is true that universal male suffrage was no longer the rule, and it is also true that frequently the old regent class was supplemented by Patriotic newcomers. Popular support, which had been strong in the first years after 1795, waned and affairs were gradually left to those in power. The theoreticians and idealists of the early days were substituted by administrators and organizers, and this was the period in which the Netherlands built up its own bureaucracy, infused by ideals of decency, incorruptibility and common sense, even though it had strong influence and power. They were, as bureaucrats, conservatives, in many ways gradualist at most, often lacking imagination and idealism. The lawyer C.F.van Maanen (1769 - 1849) belonged to this new group of industrious and clear-thinking men who now ruled the state. Lack of an imaginative personality and a strong inclination towards hiding behind the formalism that could serve all powers and masters, were compensated for by diligent work. In this way Van Maanen instituted the code of law - an orderly, clear code for the whole land - on the French model, it is true, but adapted to the typical conditions in the Netherlands. Within this group some bureaucrats had a kind of stubborn loyalty to a cause: Rutger Jan Schimmelpenninck (1761 - 1825), Grand Pensionary from 1805 to 1806, had to give up his royal position because he could not conceal his disappointment in the French handling of 'his' Republic. But perhaps more interesting were those Patriots who, as bureaucrats, at least tried by administrative reform to attain the ideals of equality and liberty they had fought for. I.J.A.Gogel (1765 - 1821), possibly the most capable of them all, introduced a radical tax reform which for the first time in the history of the Netherlands really set out to spread the burden of taxation over all citizens. J.H.van der Palm

(1763 - 1840) reformed education in the style of the Enlightenment, by means of a general law for all citizens, making school inspection obligatory. Thus the political and judicial organization of the state functioned smoothly thanks to a newly-formed civil service and centralization, which before 1798 had been such a stumbling-block. Finally, the period of French domination helped to strengthen a kind of national feeling that gradually overcame the strong deeply-rooted feelings of regional and local patriotism. In the first place this was due to the successful working of the centralized government. War weariness, paralysis of trade, the draining of all monetary reserves began to be felt, and created for the Dutch people a kind of common fate. The period of French annexation helped to exacerbate existing anti-French feelings. Compulsory military service for young men of twenty-one to twenty-four years of age stirred up bad blood. Of the 15,000 men who served under Napoleon on his march to Moscow, only a small number returned. It was not surprising that a kind of national feeling arose that found expression in thought and the arts. Poets such as Willem Bilderdijk (1765 - 1831) gave vent to these feelings in verbose verse, but better than in this emotionalized conservatism of Bilderdijk one sees this development towards national consciousness in the works of Gijsbert Karel van Hogendorp (1762 - 1834). As one of the very few of the old regent class who had not been involved in any government after 1795, he had remained a true Orangist for the greater part of this period, and he never lost complete sight of the possibilities of bringing the House of Orange back to the Republic. This was not only because of conservative stubborness. As a young man he had interested himself in modern political thought and his visit to the United States in 1783 had convinced him of the necessity of some kind of state reform in the Netherlands. Writing profusely as a spectator of what was going on in his country, he gradually worked out the frame-work of a constitution for a new kind of independent centralized state, to take effect when the French should leave. In this he decided to incorporate some of the reforms which had been worked out by the Dutch bureaucrats. At the same time he also wanted the son of Stadtholder William V (who died in exile in 1806) to return from exile and reign as the constitutional monarch. In 1813, when France finally lost her hold on the Netherlands, Van Hogendorp seemed the right person to point the way. Though pro-Orange and an aristocrat by origin and conviction, he did not have the conservative emptiness of the earlier generation of Orangists. As soon as the French troops withdrew, he began an action for the return of the House of Orange and invited a number of leading citizens to form a temporary government. This government recalled the hereditary prince William (born 1772), who on 30 November 1813 landed at Scheveningen and was received not as Stadtholder William VI but as a sovereign monarch William I.

The new government formed by its own initiative immediately cut itself off from France. For the Netherlands this had important consequences; the new sovereign state took its place among victorious nations. Thanks to this international position the Netherlands was able to retrieve not only its own independence but also a greater part of its overseas territories and, most important, to carry out the experiment of the greater reunited Netherlands.

*Six Members of the First National Assembly, 1796-'97*

# The experiment of the great kingdom

*1815 - 1839*

The plan, to which the ambitious sovereign monarch William I agreed, was of English origin. The idea was that the Netherlands, raised to the status of Kingdom, should act as counterbalance in the European balance of powers. The country was to be strengthened for that purpose, and with this aim in mind English statesmen offered the Netherlands not just the return of overseas colonies which had been temporarily occupied by English troops (with the exception of Ceylon and the Cape) but also the possibility of territorial expansion on the European continent, to take over the Southern Netherlands, the Grand-Duchy of Luxembourg and the so-called Rhine provinces. In 1815 these areas, with the exclusion of the Rhine provinces, were added to the area of the old Republic in the North and welded into one great indivisible state. For the first time since 1576 the Burgundian-Habsburg Netherlands were reunited.

In contrast to the energy and devotion of the new king to this task was the indifference and grumbling of his subjects. In the north there was fear of possible Roman Catholic supremacy, of rivalry from a reborn Antwerp and of necessary protective measures for the industries in the south which might be against the interest of northern trade and shipping. General apathy, however, enabled William, who was an enlightened authoritarian, to do what he wanted with the many bureaucrats he had inherited from the former régimes, and he paid little attention to opposing views. He followed a clearly demarcated path to develop his great state into a modern power based on three pillars of prosperity: the industrial possiblilities of the south with the rich Wallonian mining area, the revived shipping and trade of the north with its traditional experience and trade capital, and the products of a colonial empire, which could be exploited in a modern way. He considered the constitution and parliament as mere tools to shape his own powerful policy, and could not tolerate independent and critically minded men like Van Hogendorp. He preferred colourless and obedient officials, such as his capable Minister of Justice Van Maanen.

In this manner William I organized his new state with a firm hand. He continued the industralization of the south, begun during the French occupation, with great deliberation and energy, and warmly supported the improvement of transport, in the form of canals like the Zuid Willemsvaart joining the city of Liege with the navigable part of the Meuse, the North Holland canal and the canal of Voorne and Putten that gave both Amsterdam and Rotterdam better links with the sea. The first railway line between Amsterdam and Haarlem was built in 1839, the last year of his reign, and with much feverish haste various societies and institutions, trade and shipping firms were set up. The Netherlands Bank and cultural institutions like the Academy of Fine Arts and the Royal Academy of Sciences were William's creations. Of great consequence for the Southern Netherlands was his decision on the Dutch language which he ordered to be the official language of the Flemish part of the Southern Netherlands and of the second capital of the Kingdom, Brussels. In this way the Dutch language, during the French period bastardized and almost supplanted, survived in the Flemish parts of what later became Belgium.

There was one serious drawback to all these important steps taken by William I: they were all taken with too little reference to the wishes of the people, and some of these changes were bound to be against the interests of one or more groups of his subjects. For example, his rulings on language were prejudicial to the Wallonian citizens and even stirred up the Flemish population because the Hollanders (the North Netherlanders) profited from it. The Hollander had been better educated and trained for the civil service than the Flemish farmer. When the King tried to make the Roman Catholic Church one of the national churches under his command, he showed himself as an enlightened monarch to be quite logical but also extremely tactless - he only raised a storm of protest and drew back too late. Among the well-to-do citizens in the south, for long nurtured on the ideas of the French revolution and more open-minded towards French civilization than those of the north, objections began to be raised against the way the King handled affairs without listening to their opinions and views. For William I, suppression of this dangerous example of a new revolutionary Liberalism was the only solution. A strict censorship of the press and firm control over party formation seemed to him the best remedy. Perhaps the King and his bureaucracy would have easily ridden any storm, had it broken out on its own: perhaps he would have been able to prove the worth of his experiments to his northern critics, granted time. But the storms fused in one critical moment which came too early to overcome the indifference or grumblings of the north. The Wallonian liberals were inspired to action by the July revolution in Paris of 1830: demonstrations were held on the King's birthday on 28 August 1830 in Brussels. The authorities underestimated the danger: they reacted weakly and placed the responsibility for restoring order in the hands of the voluntary Civil Defence in the city, which, ironically enough, was formed by liberal-minded citizens of Brussels. This rolling stone started an avalanche: with Brussels under its control the Civil Defence began to make demands. William I showed little understanding of the situation. He promised concessions and at the same time sent troops. These remained outside Brussels at first, but then without success attempted to subdue the town (23 - 26 September). Roman Catholic help for the defence of the city started to come in. More and more Wallonians and

Flemish, gathering under the Brabant colours and giving themselves a new national name of 'Belgians', went over to the side of the Brussels rebels. On the 23rd of November 1830 the National Congress declared Belgium an independent state and excluded the House of Orange for ever from the throne.

The rebellion in the meantime threatened to develop into a civil war between the army of the Northern Netherlands and the Belgian volunteer armies. The Big Powers intervened. France was greatly interested of course in what happened north of her borders. After all, the system by which France had to be held within its boundaries was crumbling with the help of the Belgian insurgence, and hopes of possible extension and reunification of Belgium with France were nursed by a French régime that had itself recently come into power by revolution. France began first by diplomatic but very soon by military means to support Belgian resistance. England, which had taken the initiative in 1813 to bring about the union of north and south, changed her attitude, and impressed by the Belgian national resistance and irritated by Netherland's trade rivalry in the East-Indies, supported Belgium's independence contrary to France's plans of annexation. In this international game William's hand was weak. Only a few groups remained pro-Orangist in Belgium: trade circles in Ghent and Antwerp, the nobility, and some convinced Flemish nationalists who wanted to preserve the unity of all Dutch-speaking people. In the north there was a reaction of injured pride rather than of real conviction that Belgium should remain within the Dutch Kingdom. A show of military force to get the best conditions for a definite separation of the states seemed to the northerners sufficient. William I had made too individual a way for himself. Now that he was lost in the maze of internal disorder and international interference, he was supported by no one.

The only thing left to the King was to try for the most favourable solution for his smaller Netherlands. With this end in mind he argued endlessly at international conferences held in London for the settlement of borders and debts. The Dutch army, driven from Belgian territory by the French in 1832, remained for years under arms, until

William accepted terms in 1839. The border settlement was to be of immense importance for the future of the Netherlands. The former fortress towns of Maastricht and Venlo were incorporated in Netherlands territory together with Roermond in a new province of Limburg. A long time was to pass before this eleventh province (the old province of Holland was at that time split into two provinces) joined the Netherlands in spirit.

The 1839 Agreement meant for King William I the bankruptcy of his policy. Disappointed, he abdicated in 1840. His experiment had failed. It had been too much *his* experiment.

*Thorbecke*

# 20      The new basis

*1848*

The loss of the Southern Netherlands, for the second time, was hardly regretted in the north. But disappointment was felt about the apparent weakness of the nation that could be manipulated against its interests by a stubborn king and by calculating great powers who were indifferent to the wishes of the Dutch. The Belgian Revolt had two effects upon the Netherlands: it edged the country out of the mainstream of international power politics and interference for the second time, and it stimulated within the élite a feeling not just of disillusion but of the need to do something to give it back its own voice in its own affairs. The well-to-do citizens in particular had been shocked into the consciousness of their possible strength and important position within the smaller nation.

William I's efforts, sometimes helped by others, had laid the foundations for the new economic welfare: resumption of trade and exploitation of the East Indies (Java), redress of the textile industries in Twente (cotton) and improved communications (canals in particular). After 1830 there is a certain revival also of political and generally cultural consciousness. A new magazine 'De Gids' ('The Guide') took a positive lead in renewing literary and social life. E.J.Potgieter (1808 - 1875) became the skilled and consciously national man-of-letters of the Gids-group. He was critical, open-minded and above all a Liberal in spirit and action. In religious life it seemed that the straitjacket of dull dogmatism or convential moralism was coming apart. Orthodox protestants like G.Groen van Prinsterer (1801 - 1876) attempted to deepen this dogmatism not only as a means of a personal experienced elevation but also as a new way for coping with the political and social problems of society. More rigid orthodox groups, observing too much confusion and vagueness in the main Protestant Church, decided amongst themselves to set up a really 'reformed' Church in 1834, and all this despite a ban by the government, which at that time still felt it had to protect the great official Protestant Church. At the same time a more modernistic liberal-Christian trend started to develop. The Groningen movement aimed at a relatively free interpretation of the bible in an attempt to reconcile the Holy Book with modern knowledge. The most far-reaching results, particularly in England, France and Belgium, were attained by the growing political movement of Liberalism. In 1839 Johan Rudolf Thorbecke (1798 - 1872) fired his 'first shot into the sleeping forest' of the Netherlands. In his 'Remarks on the Constitution', this professor from Leiden was the first to set out concretely how, in his opinion, by a change in the existing constitution, the citizen may play a larger role in the government and administration of his country. 'The constitution should be a national force, not a formality.' Freedom, personal sense of responsibility, a balance of power between those who govern and those who are governed were the main points that Thorbecke wanted not only to be stated clearly in the constitution but also to inspire the lives of the citizens. In his plans, Thorbecke showed a remarkably good combination of idealism, strongly influenced by German Romanticism, and sober realism. Part of the old revolutionary theory of the Patriots now received greater reality and definite form. Determination, intrinsic truth and clear thinking were now injected into a democratic idea, which had lacked such qualities in 1795. After the experiences under French domination and the authoritarian rule of a King, the

Netherlands appeared to be ready for the new trend of Liberalism.

The amendments to the constitution in 1840 produced, at first, little change. William II accepted advice more readily than his father in this matter, but his advisors still belonged to the King's close circle of conservative courtiers and cautious bureaucrats. The demand of the liberal opposition for a radical change in the constitution was ignored. It is very likely that everything would have remained dormant, had not the revolution of 1848 in Italy and France, and later in Austria and Germany, so frightened the King, that he promptly changed his mind. He was stimulated to do so in particular by the revolutions in the German states where many of his relatives sat on tottering thrones. On 23 March William II switched in twentyfour hours from being a conservative to being a liberal. Though generally expected that he would, Thorbecke did not immediately receive a seat in the government, but he did sit on the commission set up to study the necessary revision of the constitution. The proposals which in the end were accepted by Parliament went a long way towards accepting Thorbecke's ideas. He then formed his own Cabinet of Ministers in 1849, which drew up and promulgated a series of laws based on the revised constitution: an electoral bill, a bill on the provinces and a municipal bill were passed in 1850 and 1851.

The new form of the constitution, as revised, was based on two ideas which had already been formulated in 1813 and 1815. The idea of a centralized state was in fact an inheritance of the French period. The recognition of a dynastic King as Head of the State stemmed from the changes in 1813. But the position of the King underwent a certain change after Thorbecke's revision. In future the King was to be above party and political divisions, a symbol of the unity of the country, and also a 'flywheel of the state machine'. He had the power to intervene, when the government found itself in an impasse, by his right to appoint the 'formateur' who had to try and set up a Cabinet of Ministers, or by his right to dissolve Parliament. On the other hand, the Ministers, and not the King, were made responsible to the Lower House (Second Chamber), directly chosen by the electorate, which received far-reaching powers of control and legislation and could call each Minister to account. The second Chamber acquired the right to initiate and amend legislation, to question the Minister ('interpellatie'), and eventually to form its committee of inquiry which could without reference of the cabinet interview people ('enquête'). Of at least equal importance were the ideals of freedom laid down as basic principles in the constitution: freedom of religion, press, education and assembly. Thorbecke also allowed for regional and local variety with the result that the Netherlands have never become an unbendingly centralized state. Provinces and municipalities had their own administration and authority whereas the central administration had only a final say. A careful balance was struck between government-appointed officials and elected bodies of control. The King and Government appointed the Governors of the Provinces ('Commissaris') and the Burgomasters of the Municipalities. The seat of control was given to the two houses of parliament, the provincial states and the municipal council, all of which (with the exception of the First Chamber, elected by the Provincial States) were directly elected. Certain safeguards were provided against possible caprices of the electors: the First Chamber was indirectly elected and was empowered to pass or reject laws only; a Council of State chosen by the King had an advisory position in the legislation.

Thorbecke was in favour of general suffrage in principle, but thought it not wise in practice to introduce it immediately. The right to vote was therefore limited to males who payed taxes above a stated minimum. This gave the right to vote to not more than 73,000 voters in population of 4 million, but Thorbecke intended a gradual extension as soon as other, less well-situated levels of the population were judged responsible enough to take a full part in political life. This idea of gradual 'democratization' showed Thorbecke's belief in the idea of the sovereignty of the people and his wise and perceptive statesmanship.

It has been an advantage to the Netherlands that modern liberal constitutional reforms were introduced *before* the process of economic and social modernization of society took place. When the industrial revolution came with all its social and cultural consequences, the modern institutions and the democratically built up system of government could cope with it. When things changed radically in society, then of course political institutions and parliamentary traditions tended to lag behind, but the distance between the one and the other was never great, and the built-in possibilities of change in the political machinery by extension of the electorate, in legislation and flexibility of the executive, smoothed relationships in political and institutional affairs. Thorbecke's merit lay in the clarity and suppleness with which he ordered the constitutional monarchy of the Netherlands. For more than a century and up to the present day the basic principles of the amended constitution of 1848 have remained the form wherein Dutch society could change and progress.

# 21    The growing importance of the colonies

*1798 - 1900*

When the two trade companies for the East and the West Indies were dissolved by the Batavian Republic, it was a matter of taking over. The companies had tried to retain their monopolies too long. Their employees had been underpaid, and misuse, corruption and even swindling had undermined everything. The books of the East India Company were closed with a deficit of 134½ million guilders. Soon after the war with England lost the Netherlands nearly all her overseas possessions, and in 1811 Java, one of the last, fell into English hands. It was not until 1813 and even later that the possibility arose for the return of the overseas possessions.

Of the areas actually returned in 1815, Java in the East Indian Archipelago above all was to become the most important island of the large colonial empire. The West Indian colonies - Surinam and the islands in the Carribean Sea (the Antilles) of which the port of Curaçao was the most important as centre of the Carribean trade - were to diminish in value. The end of the slave trade, internationally agreed to in 1815, seriously affected Curaçao. Surinam began its definite decline in 1863 with the abolition of slavery; the plantations of sugar and cotton could only be worked by the hard, forced labour of the African slaves. Surinam was to remain the Netherlands' problem-child until the present time.

The Dutch East Indies, however, increased in importance. Certain areas in Java had earlier been exploited by private effort, and following the period of English administration under Thomas Raffles (1811 - 1816), private enterprise increased and the new Dutch colonial government tried by the use of the existing land revenue laws to solve its financial difficulties. The Governor-General Johannes van den Bosch (1780 - 1844) introduced in 1830 his Cultivation Law which tried to exploit land and people in such a way that labour produce became a kind of tax on the use of land in general. The native peasant had to pay rent for the full use of his land in prescribed products he was forced to cultivate. These products were profitable on the European market, viz. sugar, coffee, tobacco, indigo etc. But for this purpose the native had to give up the best part of his land, the greater part of his time and energy, and often felt the coercion as an unjustified burden. Government officials were in control, native village chiefs were engaged to keep a check, with promises of a percentage of the profit - in fact a carte blanche permitting the village chief to extort the peasants.

Control of the Dutch East Indies was kept in government hands in the Netherlands for many years and remained outside the field of vision of the nation. The terrible Java war (1825 - 1830), when a fanatical Mohammedan revolution was put down, hardly touched public opinion. No concern was felt for a long time for the excesses of the Cultivation System, until great famines in Java in the years 1849 and 1850 gained public attention. Up till then this system was clearly advantageous to the Dutch state treasury and that was all that seemed to matter. After 1848, some members of parliament with knowledge of the situation began to protest against the excesses of the exploitation of the suffering Javanese peasant. Eduard Douwes Dekker (1820 - 1887), a discharged official of the East Indies, wrote a book (Multatuli, 'Max Havelaar', 1860), strongly protesting against the exploitation of the natives by their chiefs and princes with Dutch government sanction, which became famous. But in the end it was liberal opposition and liberal theory which gradually became more critical of what was going on in Java. Private enterprise seemed to be curbed and hindered by state intervention and state monopoly, and it was felt that free trade and enterprise would develop Java in a much better way. Some well-known young leaders in the Liberal group in Parliament started to work for the abolition of the Cultivation System and in 1870 at last the System was virtually abolished.

Now the turn had come for the private person in Java, which till 1870 had been an area for the administrator and colonial bureaucrat. The energetic, hard-working private European colonists, planters and traders, who on their own initiative introduced new products and techniques into the Indies, changed the appearance of this large area. Private enterprise could not do exactly as it liked: to protect the peasant, an Agrarian Law was passed which prohibited the sale of cultivated lands to Europeans (1870), who had to look elsewhere for fertile uncultivated land, often outside Java. From 1870 onwards the so-called outer provinces of the Dutch East Indies suddenly came into focus. Private traders and planters became interested in the great isles of Sumatra and Borneo. Soon, valuable minerals such as oil would be found and within certain regions specialized plantations arose, for example tobacco in Deli on Sumatra. The colonial government with its seat in Batavia had to follow up this private initiative and to support it. Soon the private interests of European newcomers clashed with the interests of the native population and the Government had to move in to restore order and to help the Europeans to safeguard their economic interests. Gradually, by means of many military expeditions, the outlying islands were pacified. Unfortunately several expeditions, by their cruelty in dealing with the native inhabitants, blotted the pages of colonial history. The most notorious, the Atjeh expeditions (1873 - 1904), in fact a series of long drawn-out wars, never seemed to end. Despite these drawbacks, the development of the East Indies was indeed remarkable. Railway connections were established over Java and parts of Sumatra, a wide and finely-spun net of scheduled shipping-connections between all islands came into existence (the Paketvaart Maatschappij, 1888). And everywhere the Dutch officials of the colonial government in Batavia appeared, often trying to help the native population to adapt to the situation, serving as instruments of private interests in the modernization of the country. For the first time the East Indian Archipelago became one in administration and government.

The expansion of western culture had another side to it. It brought about corresponding change in native society. When first introduced, European techniques as represented by the railways, steamboat and later automobiles amazed the inhabitants, but they soon got used to them. However, the western economic system was more difficult to appreciate.

Thrift, pleasure in work, energetic and efficient organization remained too long unknown to the local people. Abuse of human strength and work, tyranny by their own rulers and neglect or downright exploitation by the Europeans had smothered all hopes of achievement and success. Their culture often seemed to teach them satisfaction and acceptance of their lot, holding passive meditation to be the most worthy aspiration in life. But whether the native understood the changes or not, he had to go along with them and submit to the demands of ordered work and modern technique. The Dutch employer came into closer contact with the native worker than the Dutch civil servant had done in the past, though still in a position of employer towards employee, always discernible by the colour of his skin and the way he talked and behaved. Many peasants became workers on the European plantations, getting acquainted with the European in his patriarchal position of energetic, demanding 'father' figure, and in his often ruthless ambitions as an employer. Tensions were to develop which could not be avoided in this colonial relationship, but in spite of all this, modernization came to the East Indies and peace seemed to reign.

The Netherlands themselves also became strongly influenced by the East Indies, particularly after 1870. The bonds were tightened literally by better communications after the opening of the Suez Canal (1869), the improvements of the postal service and the establishment of the Netherlands Steamship Company (1870), and figuratively by closer personal and economical contacts with the Dutch overseas. New interests in anthropology and languages were encouraged by the availability of 'material' in the colonies. People travelled more often from the Netherlands to the East Indies, from the populated settled areas to the unknown forests and jungles in the East Indies. The leading firms in the Indies introduced many new East Indian products on the Dutch market such as Deli tobacco, quinine, Robusta coffee, rubber, tin and oil.

The Dutch Indies were to become one of the mainstays of Dutch economy up till 1914 or even later.

The Netherlands had shrunk to a small country in 1830, but a great empire developed overseas.

*Irrigation works in Indonesia*

*1860 - 1914*

The impression one gets from the Netherlands in the
second half of the 19th century is one of opened windows
and a fresh breeze of change and new ideas. The repeal of
the Cultivation Act for Java in 1870 was just one expression
of this improvement. It was further expressed in the
Netherlands themselves - economically,politically and
culturally. The economic sphere showed the most evident,
but in no way the only change.

The industrial revolution started after 1860. Compared with
England and France, the Netherlands were very backward
industrially. King William I had never had the full
co-operation of his people in carrying out his far-reaching
plans. Long after his reign the country remained
economically apathetic, the working classes were still
unskilled, underpaid and listless, industry was mainly
handwork and home-industry. Grass grew between the
cobblestones of the wharves in Amsterdam. There was
hardly any increase of population (4 million at the most).
Railways were known but after the connection of Haarlem
with Amsterdam not much more was done: the river barge,
and horse and waggon, were the best known means of

transport. Only a few economic developments had preceded those introduced after 1860 - the Twente and Tilburg textile industry, the Amsterdam machine industry and sugar refineries showed slow but sure growth. For two reasons, industrial modernization did not seem necessary: the colonial products imported by the Dutch government on the basis of the Cultivation System in Java assured the Dutch traders of an easy item to sell at a profit; England's urgent need for grain, dairy products and meat could easily be met by the well-developed agrarian production in the Netherlands. Only when colonial state trade seemed to slacken and in particular when American and Russian prices of grain pushed the Dutch products out of the market, were the Netherlands forced to look for other means of existence.

Development had already begun in one direction when these crises still had to teach the Dutch a definite lesson. Perhaps the most spectacular was the rapid improvement in the communications network. Private development of the railways had been almost impossible because of the marshy nature of the soil and the many waterways which had to be bridged; their construction required the expenditure of too much capital. In 1860 the Government took over. Profits from the Cultivation System in Java made it possible for the State to construct dykes and bridges. Railways now spread rapidly across the whole of the Netherlands. Completion of the Moerdijk bridge across the Hollands Diep, south of Dordrecht, measuring 2,5 km, with 14 spans, opened to traffic in 1872, was an impressive result of gathering strength. 'Out-of-the-way' provinces like Limburg and Groningen became incorporated in the Netherlands. Besides Holland, other provinces could now be opened up to industrialization and modernization. Technical improvements furthered the development of shipping. In 1863, the two large harbours of Rotterdam and Amsterdam were promised by the Government better and shorter communications with the sea. This promise was fulfilled in 1873 and 1876: Amsterdam had its North Sea canal, gigantic sluices being required at IJmuiden; Rotterdam had its Nieuwe Waterweg. The engineer Caland was successful in solving the problem of the silting up of the mouth of this waterway by making use of the regular sea tide. These improvements coincided with an increased intake of goods to both harbours: in this way, Amsterdam was able to cope with the stream of merchandise from the economically liberalized East Indies. Rotterdam became the main port for trans-shipment of industrial and raw materials exported from the rapidly industrializing Ruhr area in Germany. Shipping was modernized, steam pushed out sail, new shipping companies were founded and thanks to the free trade of those days, the Dutch became important freight shippers once again.

Money and credit became more readily available. The first attempts at modernizing banking methods, inspired by the French example of the 'Crédit Mobilier', were made shortly after 1860. The crises of 1866 and 1873 slowed down but did not halt this modernization. Modern banking and credit control were based after 1900 on these earlier foundations. The same modernization was to be found in industry, first in Twente, where a disastrous fire in 1862 called for the construction of new factories. Labourers who had previously worked at home were now concentrated in these central buildings, where a division of labour was possible and the steam engine could replace manpower. Other new branches of industry developed: in strawboard (at Leeuwarden in 1865), margarine (at Oss in 1871), and the modern clothing industry of Amsterdam. After 1890, industrialization in modern forms was speeded up and spread more rapidly: potato flour and strawboard factories in Groningen, brickmaking along the main rivers, shipbuilding in most of the harbour cities; while the manufacture of electric lamps, cigars, diamonds, etc. expanded.

Development in agriculture was slower, because for a long time it had been very profitable in its old forms, and not until the agrarian crisis of 1880 - 1895 was the need for change felt. The growth of cities and industry demanded increased production on the land and stimulated modernizaton in this field also. Cultivation of crops more suitable to the Netherlands' soil than grain crops, such as beetroot, tulip bulbs and vegetables, were new interests. With the application of a more systematic and scientific training in agriculture, considerable advances could be made in the use of artificial fertilizer, development of new crops, mechanization of agriculture. After the agrarian crisis, the farmers started to form farmers' co-operatives which specialized particularly in the handling of dairy products. Agricultural banking gave financial assistance, and the last waste lands of the country - the heath-lands in Drente and North Brabant - were made productive. The Netherlands Heath-lands Society took over the task of developping these unproductive isolated areas. In 1852 the Haarlemmermeer (lake near Haarlem) had been reclaimed, while a more ambitious plan, the reclamation of the Zuyder Zee, proposed by C. Lely, and approved by Parliament in 1918, was also intended to add to the area of arable land needed for a growing population.

Mining developed even later than agriculture. At first only a single coal-field near Kerkrade (South Limburg) was in operation, but after 1850 a few other collieries came into existence, underwritten by foreign capital. In 1901 new state-operated mines showed satisfactory results. The quality of Limburg coal was certainly not as good as Belgian or English coal and was mainly used for industrial purposes, but the production of coal had its own historical significance in another way. Economically, Limburg was at last more firmly incorporated in the Netherlands, which carried political and cultural consequences. During the Belgian Revolt in 1830, the Limburg population had preferred union with Belgium; in 1848 some wanted union with the new German federation. In 1919 Limburg emphatically stressed her satisfaction with her union with the Netherlands when Belgium expressed hopes of annexing the area. Thus it was the mining industry that gradually made Limburg into a Dutch province.

After 1890, the Netherlands were carried along in the mainstream of world capitalism.

*1848 - 1919*

The rules of the parliamentary game were drawn up in 1848, but whether the players would abide to them was another question. And if they did, would they keep to the spirit of the game? It was soon evident that King William III - William II died in 1849 and was succeeded by his son - would find it difficult to co-operate. When, as a consequence of the revised constitution by which church and state were definitely separated, Roman Catholics were allowed to introduce their occlesiastical organization in the Netherlands, William's unwillingness became evident. An 'April Movement' of indignant orthodox Protestants found a sympathetic response with the King and Thorbecke felt forced to hand in his resignation. The King, however, could do no more for 'his' party and the Roman Catholic hierarchy was restored (1853). A new Cabinet of Ministers accepted the inevitable consequences of the revised constitution.

The final decision was reached in the years 1866 - 1868, when William III attempted to retain his trusted conservative Cabinet against the wish of a majority in Parliament. Repeatedly, whenever conflict arose between

Ministers and the House, he used, on the advice of his Ministers, the expedient of dissolution of Parliament, hoping that in this way the elections would bring in representatives more favourable towards his Cabinet. Two dissolutions of Parliament within two years could not prevent each newly elected House from passing motions directed against the conservatives. Finally the King gave in and his Cabinet was dismissed. This was a triumph for the parliamentary system as such - from then onwards the King maintained no Ministers against the will of Parliament and refrained from further open interference in politics. His successors, his daughter, Wilhelmina (1890 - 1948) and his granddaughter Juliana were strictly constitutional and accepted the parliamentary rule of the majority.

In Parliament, the focal point of Dutch political life since 1848, a very lively co-operation developed between the executive (Cabinet of Ministers and their departments) and legislative (the two Chambers) powers. On the one hand this co-operation could cope flexibly with most of the needs and innovations of a continually changing society; on the other it reflected all the nuances of the social religious life of the élite in the Netherlands with its many contradictions. A certain 19th century rationalism and decency in debate governed Parliament and gave its imprint even to those parties that entered parliament in the late 19th or early 20th century, representing quite different sections of society, thanks to the extension of the franchise. If the parliamentary constitution was to be successful, it was necessary that all should conform in the belief that the virtues of reason, forbearance, freedom and decency, education, equality and progress - in fact the ideals of liberalism - should be supported and respected. Even though an 'anti-revolutionary' group and its informal leader Groen van Prinsterer rejected the ideals of the French Revolution explicitly, it adjusted itself to the idea of parliament, which by its revised constitution was clearly based on the ideas of the French Revolution. Groen's greatest service in this respect was his refusal shortly after 1848 to support the King's attempt to change the constitution in a reactionary way. Regardless of all differences of opinion, co-operative work proved to be possible because of this basis acceptance of a common style and attitude.

The parliamentary history of the Netherlands since 1848 seems to the spectator to be a rather dull and slow affair. Indeed, the characteristics of parliamentary procedure were to be serious, thorough, long-winded and cumbersome rather than quick-witted or rapidly decisive. The rules of behaviour assumed politeness and care, and it is only by carefully weighing everything said and reading between the lines that one recognizes the often deeply felt emotions and carefully prepared attacks. But on the other hand, the Dutch Parliament had the advantage of taking society and its problems seriously, of balancing different views in the most just way, and of trying to find ways out of impossible impasses by clever compromises. Also, such parliamentary procedure can get to the bottom of most questions of philosophical, religious belief.

Perhaps all this can best be illustrated by the famous 'School Question' which for more than sixty years was one of the main issues of Parliament. Here, the basic argument was about the religious education of the child. The liberals, believers in the freedom of each individual to decide for himself, after having gained knowledge and insight of the problems of life by education, wanted to secularise education so that it followed no particular denomination. The State ought to ensure that all children were offered the opportunity to attend school, and it should therefore subsidize 'general' schools ('mixed', consisting of Protestants, Catholics and Jews). The Calvinists and Roman Catholics, who put up a united front in this fight for their schools, wanted education to be in the spirit of the faith of the parents, not only in order to secure for the child a harmonious religious and intellectual life, but also to protect him from straying from the Truth and falling into false beliefs influenced by his own sinful knowledge. The right of the family as such to decide what education the children of the family should get, was considered to be a human right. Groen called this right the 'sovereignty within its own circle'. In practice this meant that private schools of all types, of different shades of Protestantism or Roman Catholicism, should not only be recognized but subsidized by the state on an equal footing.

For a long time the liberals held to their ideas and subsidized only the 'neutral' 'public' schools. Protestants and Roman Catholics had, for a long time, to pay their own way and it was only by a great deal of effort and sacrifice that these private schools were kept going. Slowly but surely the religious groups had their way. In 1889 the possibility of a subsidy for private education and schools was opened up. In 1920, complete support for private schools was given. From this time onwards, the State has been held responsible for full education for all children, but wherever a private school is founded, the State is obliged to provide an equal subsidy on condition that the school conforms to the regulations concerning building, minimum number of pupils, subjects taught, standard of teaching etc. Thus there appeared in many villages and towns and in all the cities, various Protestant (more or less orthodox etc.) and Roman Catholic schools, side by side with the state schools. Later, particularly in the larger cities, the progressive teaching methods of Montessori and Dalton, among others, had the same chance to develop due to this system of equality of state subsidies for schools. On the positive side this indeed meant a strengthening of the idea of the autonomy of the family, the intensification of the variety in beliefs and religions, the realization of true freedom in education; on the negative side, there was further disunity, dividing - more than necessary - the Netherlands into separate groups, religious sects, and classes. The school question had, moreover, far-reaching political effects. It stimulated the rise of religious political parties, forced Roman Catholics and Protestants, former enemies, to co-operate in a 'coalition' which, even after the victory in the school question, enabled Protestants and Catholics to control together the government from 1918 to 1939. The deeply religious and traditional 'confessional' parties were sometimes internally unsure or divided when interests of an economic or social nature were discussed, and this caused confusion in the general political situation. One other main problem was the extension of the franchise. Thorbecke had accepted the idea of eventual general suffrage but never made clear when he expected such a definite goal to be reached. Most liberals wished to take their time about this extension. The confessional groups and later the socialists tried from 1880 onwards to speed up this matter, aided by left-wing liberals. In 1887 and 1894 the first important extensions of the franchise were at last put into effect, but it was a long time before general suffrage became a fact: in 1917 for all men and in 1919 for all women.

Finally, a growing problem in Parliament was social legislation. The liberals regarded interference of the State in the private life of citizens, except in cases of dire necessity, as wrong. The main task of government was, in their opinion, the maintenance of order and justice and the guaranteeing of personal freedom. Only gradually had left wing liberals, from 1870 onwards, accepted the idea that in the case of abhorrent labour conditions such as child labour and bad housing , legislation should be speeded up. The confessional parties, although originally fatalistic because they were inclined to accept God's ordering of society and to explain social inequality as the inevitable outcome of God's Will, came to support the idea that state interference in social problems was acceptable and commendable. Socialists, of course, advocated complete nationalization and regarded the State as the only protector of all citizens who were fundamentally equal partners running the State.

Social evils, intensified in some backward, underdeveloped industrial areas since the Industrial Revolution, and the examples of other more progressive countries, set social legislation in motion after 1870. The bill prohibiting child labour passed in 1874, and the licensing act of 1881 were modest beginnings. In 1897 the first of a series of social laws was passed, and others followed quickly: accident insurance, housing, compulsory education and child protection laws. The first modest overall plans for social insurance were put into operation shortly before the First World War.

*1848 - 1900*

For fifty years or more the shaping of state policy in the
Netherlands was in the hands of the well-to-do bourgeoisie,
who assumed this task with rapidly developing
self-confidence and equally strong self-esteem. Liberalism,
with its belief in progress, its ideal of freedom, its faith in
reason and individualism, had given this class its ideology:
the sacred rights of private enterprise and private property
were the foundations on which to build. Perhaps
Thorbecke's second Cabinet might be considered the
high-water mark of liberalism: the laws passed by them
(1862 - 1866) were typical examples of liberal ideas based
on sober realism, combined with trust in the energy of the
Dutch people. During this administration a number of old
fashioned excise duties were revoked, easing the economic
life of private enterprise in the spirit of the liberal
Manchester school. The suggestions for improving the
connections of the great seaports with the sea showed a
belief in technical progress. The bill for secondary schools
by which Thorbecke created a new type of education,
stressing science and technical skills, kept pace with
scientific progress.

The new freedom of thought and expression guaranteed by the first articles of the revised constitution of 1848 also made scientific development possible. The international aspect of liberalism seemed to open windows towards modern development in other countries - England, France and Germany in particular. Universities arose from their prescientific slumber. Important results were obtained in the field of natural science, and the physicists Lorentz (1853 - 1928) and Van der Waals (1837 - 1923) became world-famous. The success of empirical science in its turn influenced religion and philosophy. Rationalism and materialism penetrated into philosophical theory. For the Dutch, however, the influence of modernism in the Protestant churches was even more spectacular and created excitement and opposition. Faith in the absolute truth of Christian revelation was undermined by scholarly research. Analysis of the Bible showed the Holy Book to be composed of histories with a different degree of trustworthiness. Comparison with other religions caused some to see Christianity as just one of the many world religions of equal status. A kind of liberal Protestantism spread its wings within the largest Dutch Reformed Church (de Hervormde Kerk) which no longer accepted the official dogma and even became anti-dogmatic. Some ministers resigned because of their loss of faith, others created enlightened communities of modern faith (e.g. the 'Vrije Gemeente', 1878). Many Dutch citizens in the great cities lost the habit of church-going, even without the influence of socialism.

In the meantime, scientific revival in the universities brought the Netherlands back into the mainstream of thought and knowledge in Europe. In law, medicine, linguistics, history, social anthropology, theology and philosophy, Dutch contributions began to count once again. By virtue of political freedom, and the energetic development of free trade, by a conscious acceptance of the new forward drive, the Dutch bourgeoisie had reached the highest peak of scientific ability by the end of the 19th century.

In cultural life the same trends could be found. Soon after 1848 a kind of nostalgia for the 'good old days' seemed to stimulate new energy and new creative work. The Golden

Age was studied with more than just scientific curiosity. The old period of citizens' triumph was to inspire the new age. The two great historians R.C.Bakhuizen van den Brink (1810 - 1865) and Robert Fruin (1832 - 1899) tried to recreate with their critical ingeniousness and imaginative power a picture of the great times of the Dutch Revolt and the Golden Age. This same endeavour is to be found in the interest which now flourished for old monuments and museums. In 1873 it was decided to start the construction of the Rijksmuseum in Amsterdam. The art of painting, which had never been completely forgotten, was rediscovered, and Rembrandt received due recognition. The antiquarian trade in books and paintings became an important branch of commerce. In the creative art this revival of historical interests inspired architects to build in neo-Gothic style. P.J.H.Cuypers (1827 - 1921) was the builder of the Rijksmuseum and the Central Station (1889) in Amsterdam and they both look like Gothic castles with no indication of their purpose.

Soon this historical approach of renewal and revival was replaced by modernism in the creative arts. Individualism, so typical for the liberal bourgeoisie, permeated art and freed the artist from strict rules and the following of historical examples. French impressionism, the personal interpretation of one's own direct impressions of atmosphere, colours and beauty, began to appeal to the Dutch painters, who broke the bonds of tradition, and protested against the bourgeois world they came from. They followed the French example of a bohemian kind of life and Paris became for these Dutch artists the centre of culture. An impressionist school developed which soon became internationally famous. The first generation, around 1870 (known often as the 'Hague School'), applied impressionistic inspiration to paintings of Dutch landscape (Jozef Israels, Maris, Mauve etc.). A second generation, after 1870, more often turned to city life and portraiture (Breitner, Witsen, Verster). The painter who was to become world-famous after his death, Vincent van Gogh (1852 - 1897) belonged to this second generation, but he was a self-taught complete individualist, probably far more influenced in his later life by what he saw and learned in France than by his early experiences in the Netherlands.

His social protest was such that his art must be linked with the emancipation movement rather than with the triumph of the bourgeoisie in power.

Liberal individualism also stimulated literature. In the critical work of C. Busken Huet (1826 - 1886), influenced by French culture, there is a constant undertone of protest; in the lively and well-written prose of E. Douwes Dekker (1820 - 1887) this protest poured out from all sides. His famous and impressive novel 'Max Havelaar' was followed by a series of essays which dealt with the immediate problems he saw in his society and his country. The 'Movement of the 80s', through its periodical Nieuwe Gids (New Guide), tried even more consciously than its predecessors to break away from tradition and smugness. These younger poets, with their reverence for the beauty of words, their violent protest against the moralising of their predecessors, their super-individualism, had a great influence and made a deep impression. The art of the poet Willem Kloos (1856 - 1938), though soon outdated by hollow word-use and empty vowel-sound, gave nevertheless the impetus to a truly new experience of beauty.

In political life, this individualism often led to differences and divisions. The Liberals refused for a long time to form a strong party and when at last they decided to organize themselves in this way it was impossible to think of one party only. Left-wing Liberals first, and later the Liberal Democrats, repeatedly had to draw away from the more conservative elements. The violent dispute about the extension of the franchise finally produced a separate left-liberal party, which lasted until 1945: the 'Vrijzinnig Democratische Bond' (Liberal Democratic Union 1900). This weakness of individualism was also, however, its strength. The well-to-do citizens could afford the luxury of genuine interest in the problems of others, their rationalistic and moral approach to problems forced them to see the evils and weaknesses of their society and some of them were realistic enough to realize that their interests were not the exclusive interests of society, that other classes had their rights and problems and should gradually be granted the equal rights of full citizenship they themselves enjoyed. Many Liberals, though not all, had the fortitude to adapt themselves to the new demands of the times, even when, for example, general suffrage would mean that their strength in Parliament would be undermined or when social legislation would imply a kind of state interference, which they disliked in principle and in practice. A good example of this sensible adaptation were the tax reforms introduced by the Liberal N.G.Pierson. Himself a rich man, he was fully conscious of the fairness of an income tax he drew up and made into law in 1896. And thanks to his kind of adaptation to changing times, the bourgeois style of life continued to influence Netherlands society at a time when the liberal parties had become a small minority in Parliament.

Against all these 'credits' there was naturally a debit side, as was only to be expected in a class that had to protect and preserve its own strength and influence against increasing odds. The unbending personality of Thorbecke often gave an impression of high-handedness which could irritate and spoil the atmosphere: too long these citizens remained impervious to many events and changes outside their own circle. Very few actually knew of the desperate conditions of the working classes, and when they knew they could be harsh and hard. They had not much time for church and religion outside social usefulness and their thinking could be superficial and matter-of-fact. Moral life was dominated by hypocritical Victorianism.

And yet a strong, hard core of certainty steered the country, and the ideal of freedom, secured by the revised constitution and borne out by many measures over the years, opened up the country to many new external and internal trends. The Netherlands were alive again because the bourgeoisie were at the helm.

# 25     The great emancipations

*1870 - 1914*

In this rapidly developing Dutch society of the second half of the 19th century, other classes and groups formed. While the liberal bourgeoisie was in fact in power and formed the élite of the country, the middle and lower classes, underprivileged and discriminated against in the past, began to become conscious not only of their own unjust position in society, but of the possibility of organizing themselves and using the freedom of the press, of assembly and association to put pressure upon the executive to take their interests and wishes into account. The school question aroused the orthodox Calvinist section of the population. Their Church had been the most privileged and the only recognized Church in the 17th and 18th centuries, but even during that period clerics were held at bay by the regents, and the churchpeople were mainly 'petits bourgeois', craftsmen and shopkeepers, or labourers and paupers. Probably they had nominally formed the majority (just over 50 per cent) of the total population in the Republic, but many of the members of the Church had not been really active. In the 19th century this Dutch Reformed Church sustained many shocks. In the first place they had to accept the definite separation of Church and State, which resulted in the Dutch Reformed Church, being one of the more important churches, but nonetheless only one of them. In the second place the liberal 'bourgeois' who had traditionally belonged to the Church lost interest in the vital issues of dogma and organization, although it took a long time before they actually left the Church, towards the end of the 19th century. In the third place, the Church seemed to loose coherence and strength internally. Orthodox and liberal Protestants were divided on many matters; modernism seemed to undermine accepted beliefs, the traditionalism and indifference of many nominal members weakened the core of the Church. As a reaction, the more orthodox Calvinists formed a movement which gradually grew into a power of political, social and religious significance.

Groen van Prinsterer (1801 - 1876), started the movement while its spiritual and theoretical leader, Abraham Kuyper (1837 - 1920) put it on a solid basis. Through Kuyper's strong will and energy, his lively journalistic activity and his political abilities, the Anti-Revolutionary Party, founded in 1878, was firmly anchored. Kuyper realized that he would find his support among the 'kleine luyden' - the 'petits bourgeois' - a term he had coined. Using biblical language and in a pious, strongly orthodox mood, Kuyper appealed to these 'small men' - craftsmen, shopkeepers and farmers. Willingness to work together with a strong feeling of independence engendered by their own efforts, and the deeply-felt religious convictions of Calvinism, helped to weld these middle-class people together.

The emancipation of the Calvinist groups was not only a political act, it had spiritual and social consequences as well. The orthodox, disappointed with the modernistic trends of the great Reformed Church ('Hervormde Kerk') broke away from it (the so-called 'Doleantie', 1886) and founded, together with the non-conformists of 1834, a New Reformed Church ('Gereformeerde Kerk', 1892). Kuyper, who was one of the leaders of this break-away movement, wished to give it a scientific basis. He founded the Free University ('Vrije Universiteit') in Amsterdam, 1880, as a bulwark for orthodox Calvinist intellectualism.

Emphasis also remained on the orthodox private schools

and even an orthodox Protestant workers' union was created in order to keep the Protestant labourers within the fold of the Dutch Calvinist community.

As a result of all these new activities fostered by the stubborn but sometimes too self-confident Kuyper, tensions within the group inevitably arose. Dogmatism and a strong belief in the only Truth often breed intolerance and narrow-mindedness. Kuyper's friend and co-worker, A.F.de Savornin Lohman (1837-1924), finally broke away from the Anti-Revolutionary Party in 1894, and eventually formed a separate Protestant party, the Christian Historical Union ('Christelijk Historische Unie') in 1908. This party's membership almost equalled that of the Anti-Revolutionary Party, from which it differed in many ways. Most supporters of the Christian Historical Union were the more traditionally minded, who had remained within the great Reformed Church, socially often of upper-middle class origin, and tending in political and social matters to be more conservative and more firmly anti-catholic than their anti-revolutionary counterparts. Despite these divisions and troubles the Protestant church, school, union and party organizations have succeeded until this very day in binding together a great part of the active Protestants (about 20 per cent of the total Dutch population) and keeping them relatively separate from other groups.

The Roman Catholic movement took somewhat longer to develop. Not until 1853 had they achieved emancipation: previously they had been considered second-class citizens within a Protestant state, free to worship as they wanted but discriminated against in more subtle political and social ways. The agrarian provinces of Limburg and northern Brabant with their predominantly Catholic population were economically and socially in many ways more backward than the other provinces of the Netherlands: poor cottagers on the land, poor labourers in the industrial centres of Tilburg and Maastricht. For many years during the 17th century these areas had been contested territories between the Dutch rebels and loyal counter-reformatory forces in the south. And later during the 17th and 18th centuries they had been treated as conquered lands by the other provinces of the Republic. The emancipatory attempts after 1795 had been frustrated by French domination and later by the Belgian Revolt. Little wonder that the first leaders in the Catholic movement came from the Catholic minorities in the north, for example J.A.Alberdingk Thijm (1820 - 1889), supported gradually by small farmers and the lower middle classes under the leadership of the clergy.

The first impetus came from Rome. A papal bull passed in 1853 restored the official hierarchy in the Netherlands and made Utrecht an archdiocese. The Pope was strongly opposed to liberalism in his message of 1864 and encouraged Dutch Catholics to join forces with the Protestants in the school question. The encyclical 'Rerum Novarum' of 1891 stimulated social action among the Catholic workers in the Netherlands. For most Dutch Catholics Rome was the real directing and inspiring power, and with more devotion and eagerness than their brother Belgians, Germans or French, they listened to the encouragements and admonitions which came from the Head of the Church. They were also much more dutiful in church attendance, in confession, and in taking the sacraments, and Dutch convent life flourished till well after 1945. Perhaps Rome had no better, more obedient and loyal Catholics anywhere else.

But of course, this could only be decisive if within the Netherlands the Catholic organization developed with the help of native Dutch leaders. Two important men who played a role in this emancipation were the priests H.A.M.Schaepman (1841 - 1903) and Alfons Ariëns (1860 - 1928). The former founded the Catholic Political Party (the 'Roomsch-Katholieke Staatspartij') which got its name just after the death of Schaepman, in 1904. Schaepman was one of the leaders who united Catholics and Protestants in the fight for subsidies for the private confessional schools, and his championing of the extension of the franchise and social legislation in favour of the working class often put him to the left of the Catholic political groups. The Catholic State Party, however, because of its religious basis, could never become a socially homogenous party; in religious matters it was always firmly united, but in political or social matters it was frequently divided into right-and left-wing tendencies, though there never was a complete split. The curate from

Enschede, Ariëns, tried to put in practice the 'new matters' mentioned in the papal letter. Ariëns organized his Catholic Labour Movement of textile workers in the Roman Catholic industrial area of Twente. This was the beginning of a Roman Catholic workers' union which was to spread its wings all over the Netherlands after 1900.

In the end, Roman Catholic emancipation was even more successful than its Protestant counterpart. Inner discipline was very strong, and the occasional friction between the left and right wings of the party never created the rifts suffered by the Protestants. Moreover, nearly every dutiful Catholic supported his Party (70 to 80 per cent of all Dutch Catholics voted for their party up till the 1960s), and sent his children to a Catholic school, and most social clubs and sporting events had a separate Catholic organization of specific Catholic stamp. The crowning spire on this impressive tower was the Roman Catholic University at Nijmegen, founded in 1923. Finally, the proportion of Catholics has Increased, because atheism or indifference made the Protestant churches lose many members. In 1899, 35 per cent of the total Dutch population was Roman Catholic, 48 per cent belonged to the Reformed ('Hervormde') Church and 15 per cent to the new reformed churches ('Gereformeerd'). Since then, the Protestants have lost members to the non-churchgoing group which increased from 2 per cent of the total population in 1899 to 14 per cent in 1960. In 1960, the proportion of Roman Catholics in the total population (thanks to the large families of Dutch catholics) had risen to 40 per cent, while the Dutch Reformed (Hervormde) Church decreased to 28 per cent and the new Reformed Churches to 10 per cent of the total population.

The emancipation of workers followed that of Protestants and Catholics. The Industrial Revolution had not been under way for long when the first small labour organizations of a Marxist or French socialist type appeared (1870). Skilled labourers were the first to organize trade unions on a socialist and non-denominational basis (diamond workers and printers), but not long after, Marxist influence with a strong German emphasis began to appear. Ferdinand Domela Nieuwenhuis (1846 - 1919) became the idealistic prophet of this new socialist movement. Domela

Nieuwenhuis himself came from the bourgeois class, had studied theology and became a minister in the Reformed Church, but lost his faith and left the Church, becoming a committed socialist first, an anarchist later. He was the first social-democrat to enter Parliament in 1887. Political agitation in the 1880s in particular, strikes, demonstrations and riots, forced Parliament to make concessions, and the extension of the franchise and social legislation were helped by this pressure of rising Socialism. As with Protestant emancipation, contradictions and tensions also arose in this new Socialist movement. Domela Nieuwenhuis soon lost his following when he tried to remain the individualistic leader of a movement that was in need of more discipline and less vague anarchistic ideals. More politically able personalities like P.J.Troelstra (1860 - 1930) tried to channel the workers' interest in a social democratic party which attempted to reach its socialistic goals via Parliament and general suffrage rather than by revolution or anarchism. This SDAP, founded in 1894, proved to be such a success, that already in 1913 the entry of socialists into the Cabinet was taken into consideration by the other parties. But the radical-revolutionary traditions of Socialism were still too strong to accept at that stage a compromise with the bourgeois parties. The big railway strike of 1903 showed the strengh of revolutionary feeling, although the great general strike as such failed. Gradually the SDAP came to embrace evolutionary rather than revolutionary ideals. Earlier than other socialist parties in the world, the Dutch social democrats felt compelled to expel the more revolutionary elements from the SDAP in 1909; these expelled radicals became the founders of the Dutch Communist Party (CPN) in 1918.

The achievements of the Labour movement since 1880 command admiration. In education, temperance, youth-work and trade unionism, Socialism helped to lift the workers to a level of organization and power within a few decades. A desire for knowledge, need for companionship and political consciousness inspired these workers. The fight against 'Capital, King, Church and Pub' (Kapitaal, Koning, Kerk en Kroeg, the four K's) - held them together. Estrangement of the Church and religion in general was the natural result, and this again made it impossible for a long time to bring the socialist, Protestant and Roman Catholic workers together in one union or even into close co-operation. The socialist trade union movement considered the 'confessional' workers' unions as tools in the hands of the middle classes, as instruments for strike breaking and feeble compromise. Because the Protestant and Roman Catholic workers had their own strong organizations, started at the same time as the socialist ones, the labour movement remained divided for generations to come and the socialists were never successful enough to reach a strong majority within the labour class or in Parliament.

Yet another emancipation deserves to be mentioned - the emancipation of women. As elsewhere in Western Europe, women concentrated on the fight for the right to vote. If women had the vote, equality between the sexes would be reached in principle. Aletta Jacobs (1854 - 1929) was one of the most enthusiastic and intelligent advocates of women's rights. She had been the first woman to enrol at the University in 1871 and succeeded in getting her degree in medicine despite mockery and opposition. The struggle drew to a formal close in 1919 when women received the right to vote, and the women's movement petered out. Politically it had followed existing party lines and socially equality was never completely achieved. Women's liberation met with a great deal of resistance not just in the more conservative circles, but also with the confessional parties who considered women as subordinate to men as the Bible prescribed, and even with socialist working men who saw in demands for equal pay and rights for women a danger of competition of woman-labour on the labour market. Aletta Jacobs herself channelled her medical knowledge to help propagate the practice of birth control.

All these new freedoms inspired contemporary art. Some artists began to devote themselves to the service of the community rather than follow liberal individualism, to create a kind of community art with a message and a purpose. Vincent van Gogh is a typical transition figure in this development. An individualist to the core, impressionism and expressionism inspired him to find a completely independent and isolated way to solve his artistic problems, while putting his art at the service of social protest and later of general anti-bourgeois protest, against the emptiness of the outer world, from which his own soul suffered so cruelly. The period he spent in North Brabant, where he depicted the hard life of the poor cottagers, his years in the Borinage (in Belgium) showing the misery of the Belgian miners, were later followed by his French period, one of bewildered bitterness of mind but of clarified beauty.

After van Gogh, however, community art was pursued more wittingly. Herman Gorter (1864 - 1927) and Henriëtte Roland Holst (1869 - 1952), both internationally famous radicals in the communist movement, wrote their socialist message in verse. Herman Heyermans (1864 - 1924), the only playwright in the Netherlands of standing, made his dramas a realistic protest against capitalism and miserable labour conditions. But perhaps the most impressive successes were reached in the applied arts, which attempted to help the labourer not only to better but to beautify his environment. Large sculptures and leaded windows depicted allegorically the coming liberation of the working class. New public buildings and particularly new working-class houses were built, in which architects tried to be both conscious of beauty as well as practical and cheap by a kind of 'honest' construction. Following the ideas of William Morris and John Ruskin, an attempt was made to revive craftmanship. The architect H.P.Berlage (1856 - 1934) became famous for his building of the Amsterdam Stock Exchange (1904), a symbol of capitalism, and rightly so because it was one of the first buildings which tried to break way from older neo-styles and did not shirk showing functionally how the building was structured technically. At that time, this caused a sensation. His further architectural work, however, was often done in the service of the socialist creed he so strongly believed in.

Indeed it was a fruitful period, this second 'Golden Age' of the Netherlands between 1880 and 1914.

# 26     The colonial problem

*1900 - 1945*

In this time of change, when the fortune-seeking conqueror and trader in the colonies was no longer an unquestioned ruler, there arose between the native races and the Europeans the great problem of the relationship of the colonizer to the colonized. As early as 1870, steps had been taken under the Agrarian Law of that year to protect the indigenous population from unrestrained exploitation by European private enterprise. Perhaps one can consider this law as the first step taken towards a different type of colonial government. The Government saw that it was not only responsible for developing an orderly and well organized state, but also for the interests of the colonized who were due for a share in the fruits of increasing wealth. C.Th.van Deventer published his article 'A Debt of Honour' in the periodical 'De Gids' in 1899. He argued that following a successful 'education' and a general raising of the economic and social life of the native population, self-government could be granted in the long run. To allay objections on the grounds of insufficient financial means to carry out such an undertaking, he proposed that the many millions of guilders of profit which in earlier decades had poured into the Netherlands Treasury, should be returned to an East Indian treasury to be used for this specific purpose. Only in this way could the debt of honour, owed by the Netherlands to the East Indies, be repaid. And indeed this so-called 'ethical policy' became the program of many Dutch cabinets to come. The first reimbursement for this 'debt' of forty million guilders was granted in 1905 but was never followed up. On the other hand, it is true to say that since 1870 the Dutch Government has had to supply the colonial budget each year with several millions, and when the Indies' finances were at last separated from the Dutch treasury (1912) the colonial deficit always had to be paid by the Dutch Government. This did not mean of course that the Indies were an economic loss, but the profits went into the pockets of private enterprise instead of the State as had happened before 1870.

Science was brought in to help colonial administrations. C.Snouck Hurgronje (1857 - 1936) with his great knowledge of the Islamic and Arabic languages, devoted careful studies to the religious life and customs of the Atjeh tribes in North Sumatra. Only with the help of such knowledge was the Government able after 1904 to put a stop to the recurring guerrilla warfare. Studies of the many languages in the Indies and the ethnology of the various tribes also proceeded C. van Vollenhoven (1874 - 1933) studied the adat (customary law) of the native population and with some success championed respect for this adat to avoid clashes and sudden disturbing changes. The problem for the administration was whether western influence should be restrained from penetrating too rapidly into the civilizations of the many peoples on the islands, or should be encouraged. Resistance to western influence would make the gap between the European colonizer and the colonized peoples all the greater and force the administration to erect an artificial barrier, a kind of 'apartheid', between the westerner and the asiatic. Encouragement of western influence might upset society, leave the indigenous civilization in a void or even destroy the cultures still alive in the archipelago. The Government followed a middle course. Gradual change by western influence was accepted as an unavoidable way of modernizing colonial society, but at a pace which would not be upsetting or disturbing. The question remained whether time would be on the side of a colonial administration which proceeded with this kind of very slow gradualism.

In the meantime, the Government immediately attacked the most urgent problems with western methods. The rapid increase in population in Java (1815: 5 million, 1806: 11 million, 1900: 28 million, 1942: 48 million) forced the Government to act, although the problem was practically insurmountable. Irrigation was modernized in order to increase production of the ricefields, emigration of the Javanese to the less densely populated areas outside Java was encouraged, different crops and small industry were encouraged to guarantee employment. But all this did not solve the problem, and the standard of living of the individual Javanese tended to go down in the course of the decades after 1900. A major problem for the Dutch colonial administration was also the absence within this densely populated Javanese area of a middle class of shopkeepers and craftsmen; this function was performed by foreign minorities such as Chinese traders and Indian shopkeepers. The Government tried to protect the poor peasant class from usury and pauperism by setting in motion a widely spread system of small credit. In bad harvests these credit banks paid in the form of food and goods rather than in money. At least as impressive was the medical service which was organized after 1900 and extended all over the archipelago. Diseases such as tuberculosis, syphilis and framboesia were combatted with a great deal of success; epidemics such as bubonic plague seemed to have been stamped out. The common disease of beri-beri (lack of certain vitamins in husked rice) completely disappeared for a while, thanks to Christiaan Eykman's discovery of the vitamin-containing properties of rice in the husk. Although the rapid growth of the population had started much earlier and must be explained by the proletarianisation of the Javanese population in the course of exploitation by the Cultivation System, and the increase of money exchange and migration during the 19th century, it is equally true to say that in the 20th century, until 1942, the Dutch colonial medical service helped many Javanese to live longer and to survive many diseases.

Besides this care for the physical health of the population, attention had to be given to education. This was not carried out on so extensive a scale as the other social measures. In fact the pace was so slow that intentional holding-up of reforms was suspected. Some Indonesian nationalists started to build up their own school system in order to cope with the problem of illiteracy. The Colonial government tried to encourage each small village community to form a community school (the so-called dessa-school) where, however, teaching was very elementary. Illiteracy, it is true, began to disappear, but only a minority progressed beyond the most simple ability to read and perhaps write. In 1940 there were 18,000 village schools with about 2 million pupils, half the number of children of 6 to 10 years of age who should have been attending school. On the other hand, the Government helped the occasional intellectual generously by granting scholarships; a college was founded in Batavia for lawyers and in Bandung for engineers, and facilities existed to obtain a university education in the Netherlands. But for these few intellectuals it proved very difficult on their return home to find employment consistent with their knowledge and capacity. There was no 'apartheid' in the East Indies, but at the same time the European community was quite separate and the best jobs were reserved for its members.

The Government had also made known proposals for future self-government, but here too progress was very slow. In 1916, a National Council to assist the colonial government ('Volksraad') was set up in Batavia, composed of appointed and elected members, but fulfilling only an advisory function. After 1927, this Council was empowered to take some part in legislation. Care was taken that a majority of the council members should be native-born, although Europeans were over-represented on a proportional basis. Disturbing influences, especially after 1929, slowed down this already sluggish development.

One of these disturbing influences was of course the severe economic crisis which from 1929 onwards hit the Indies as a country producing mainly primary products and raw materials. Another disturbance was the Communist unrest during the '20s which even led to some serious revolts which had to be put down. But the main problem for the Dutch Colonial government was the upsurge of nationalism among Indonesians, as the indigenous leaders of the movement in the East Indies called themselves. The Japanese victory over Russia (1905) and the development of Indian nationalism under Ghandi influenced Indonesian nationalism very strongly. At first this Indonesian nationalism was certainly not anti-Dutch, but with the passing of the time, when it was realized that development was too slow, that the Javanese problem of over-population had not been solved and the gulf between Europeans and Indonesians not bridged, the nationalist parties gained more influence and became more radical themselves. The First World War, which more than ever before directed the attention of the Indies towards America and Asia, the Russian Revolution, the economic crisis - these were some of the disturbing factors which stimulated the radicalism of the nationalists.

And while this nationalism veered away from the Dutch, it seemed that the Colonial Government became more and more removed from the Indonesians, quite contrary to the intention of the 'ethical policy'. The Government favoured solidarity with Dutch economic interests, arguing of course that this could bring prosperity to the Indies. A typical example of this favouritism was tax policy, which for too long left the wealthy European firms untouched while over-taxing the population. The economic crisis was fatal for the export partnership between the Netherlands and the Indies. And under these difficult circumstances the Colonial government decided not to allow a too radical nationalist movement and took firm measures of suppression against any political expression or sign of what smelled of Indonesian nationalism.

The outbreak of the Second World War seemed at last to bring about a relaxation of tension and a certain improvement of relations between nationalists and Colonial government. The common fear of a possible Japanese invasion made for happier contacts. But the attack on the Netherlands East Indies, unavoidable after Pearl Harbour (7 December 1941) brought all this to an abrupt end. The defeat and humiliation of the Europeans in the Indies (capitulation was on March 1942) on the one hand, collaboration by some radical Indonesian nationalists with

the Japanese conquerors (e.g. Sukarno) on the other,
were the sad prelude to the coming disintegration of the
Netherlands East Indies in 1945 and after.

*Granting of Independancy to Indonesia*

# 27     Carried along in the international whirlpool

*1914 - 1940*

It would appear that the years following 1914, compared to those preceeding it, lack drive and colour. The period from 1914 till 1940 had the greyness, the drabness of a phase beginning and ending with a great war. Then there was the problem of the economic depression. More than ever before the Netherlands were affected by these world events. It is true that the country was spared the First World War, but inevitably the neutral island in a sea of hostilities was not only in constant risk of involvement, but suffered many concomitant consequences and could not turn a blind eye on the gruesomeness of a war fought so near its borders. Moreover, four years of mobilization of the army, aid to Belgium and refugees, rationing of food, heavy taxes, shipping paralysed by mines and submarines, though of smaller importance than the catastrophes suffered by less fortunate neighbours, were bad enough in the eyes of the people.

The victory of the allies brought new problems. Belgium demanded the revision of the 1839 treaty and indicated its wish to annex Zeeland-Flanders (Zeeuws Vlaanderen) and

South-Limburg. Demonstrations in these parts of the country in favour of the Netherlands helped to stave off this move (1920). For a time the asylum granted to the fleeing German Emperor was a difficult political problem.

The Netherlands had to sail through the international storms as best as it could. As in other countries, so in the Netherlands a wish for peace was interpreted as pacifism and a drive for disarmament. A bill to expand the navy unchained a series of protests and street demonstrations and brought such pressure to bear on representatives in Parliament that the bill was rejected by the Second Chamber (1923), a clear indication of the general pacifist mood. Only after 1933 did pacifism begin to wane, under the growing fear of Hitler Germany, but even then it took time before all parties dropped their hostility towards Dutch military defence.

The economic crisis of 1929 hit the Netherlands in 1931. Suddenly, within a year, the country reached a pitch of misery which it only seemed to get over after 1937. Particularly severe was unemployment in 1934: 400 to 500,000 in a population of 9 million, which by 1936 had reached 800,000. There was also a disturbing fall in prices and a severe collapse in shipping and trade. The Government, a Protestant-Roman Catholic combination, attempted to tide over this bad period by economizing, and only worsened the situation.

And in the midst of these depressing economic events, the menace of National Socialism arose in Germany. Hitler, who with every deed of aggression proclaimed his love for peace, began to stifle Europe. National Socialism seemed initially attractive to the most discontented elements in all classes and groups of the population, and especially to those who had no strict protection within an existing party or organization. Most Protestants, Roman Catholics and Socialists remained loyal to democracy: the floating vote drifted towards National Socialism. In the 1935 elections the Dutch National Socialist Movement (NSB) won more than 8 per cent of the votes, but its success was but temporary and in the last elections before the war in 1939 it did not attract more than 3 per cent of the votes. Whether this proves that the Dutch people as a whole expected a coming war with Hitler Germany is, however, doubtful. Like most other nations, many expected that at least their country would be left in peace. The Netherlands after all had managed to avoid commitment in the First World War. Why should it not escape a second time? The Netherlands had never given any pretext for Hitler to attack and it was thought that Germany would gain no advantage in attacking. The economic crisis moreover drew much more worried attention and the Dutch people tended to withdraw in the shell of its own misery. The dislike of the NSB, evinced by the great majority of voters, was rather simple decency and aversion to the warlike aggressions Hitler and Mussolini were organizing elsewhere. In 1936 rearmament began. Even the parties most opposed to militarism, the socialists and liberal-democrats, abandoned their traditional position and supported this action. The outbreak of the Second World War in September 1939 found people thinking that history would repeat itself: the Netherlands declared its neutrality and mobilized, action on the Western Front was in a stalemate, and the Dutch Government did its best to make all belligerent parties aware that this country would keep to its strict neutrality. On the 10th of May 1940 the illusion that the Dutch people would escape once more was shattered.

Internal worries seemed to absorb everyone's energy before this major catastrophe. More than ever before, now that universal suffrage was a fact, the voters left parliamentary business to party leadership and their representatives in Parliament. The new electoral system of 1917 had replaced the old district system by one based on proportional representation. Theoretically this was the most honest electoral system possible, but it was this very perfection that killed it. 'Landslide' elections were no longer possible - links between electors and elected were broken. The 30 seats out of a total of 100 in the Second Chamber belonging to the Catholics could at the most increase or diminish by one, so it seemed. The 22 for the SDAP remained constant, 23 Protestant seats shifted but slightly between the different Protestant parties. Thus a combination of different parties into one Cabinet was the only solution for a workable government, supported by a majority in Parliament. Catholics and Protestants almost inevitably worked together, while the SDAP and the smaller liberal parties were most of the time in opposition. Parliamentary life seemed to become immobilized by the unchanging political situation where the great parties held all power in their hands. Desperate attempts were made by smaller parties to obtain some influence. The elections of 1933 saw 53 parties contesting, and at least eleven parties were represented in Parliament (often by one man only). The true experts were now in Parliament, no longer the great inspiring party leaders. Even the anti-revolutionary H.Colijn (1869 - 1944), Prime Minister during the period of the economic crisis and regarded in the 1937 elections as a 'strong man', was nothing more than an energetic man with fixed ideas. He could not be compared with a Thorbecke, a Kuyper or Troelstra.

Still, it does not do to paint this period too darkly. Economically, the Netherlands certainly went ahead. Prior to 1931 this development had been expansive, after 1931 it was more intensive. Great industries grew and flourished up till 1931 and then began to rationalize and economize after 1931, for example Philips in Eindhoven, Unilever, the AKU (rayon) and the Royal Dutch Petroleum Company. The Royal Dutch Airlines (KLM), founded in 1919, became one of the main airlines in Europe. Reclamations in the Zuyder Zee continued. In 1932 the long dyke connecting the provinces of Holland and Friesland was completed and made the Zuyder Zee one great lake (the IJsselmeer). The work of reclaiming land in this lake could then be started. The Wieringermeerpolder was completed before 1940 and the North East polder, already in an advanced stage just before the war, could be settled in 1941.

The economic depression had to be met by the emergency measures of a government which disliked such steps and only hoped they would be temporary. Controlling bureaux for putting agricultural and industrial production and external trade on a kind of quota system were set up. These new methods, whether the Government wished it or not, introduced a form of economic planning which could be continued during and after the war, and then with greater impetus with the belief in its necessity and desirability. Rationalization of industry was completed during the depression: experts even spoke of a kind of 'second industrial revolution'.

Before 1931, some social problems were tackled and social conditions seemed to be improved. In 'red' Amsterdam, Alderman F.M.Wibaut (1857 - 1935), a social-democrat, worked hard to show what socialism could achieve. The construction of large working class areas and the clearing of slum areas in the city set an international example: there was an air of tidiness and businesslike activity.

Functionalism in architecture was perhaps the best reflection in the arts of this tendency. The so-called 'stijl' group of architects gave a lead with its functional furniture and designs for buildings. The cubism of P.Mondriaan (1872 - 1944) seemed to match this same energetic sobermindedness.

It is very difficult, and in fact not permissible, to try to bring all creative cultural activities under the name of functionalism. Especially after 1914, cultural life seemed to be refracted into a band of bright colours with a great deal of variety and with a tempo of change which sometimes bewildered the contemporary. Monumental paintings, neo-realism, expressionism seemed to be there at the same time, coming and going; in one person's work a whole series of styles could develop. Moreover, modern traffic greatly increased the international exchange of one's ideas and many artists knew more of what was done in Germany and France than in their own country. Cosmopolitanism in the arts was typical.

Perhaps there was yet another common characteristic of the arts. Under the threatening and darkening world of economic crisis and wars, a dark undertone could be seen in everything that found expression in different artistic forms and shapes. Seriousness, pessimism and political criticism began to replace the feelings of the 1920s. Jan Sluyters' painting of Don Quixote as a tragic figure on his decrepit horse in front of a dark sombre sky was symbolical for the year 1939, when it was painted. The brittle, careless verse of J.J.Slauerhoff (d. 1936) showed a bitter sensitivity, with no half measures. Menno Ter Braak's intelligent essays reflected in his sharply biting way the worries about the threat of National Socialism just as the prophetic plaintive work of the historian J.Huizinga (1874 - 1945) 'In the Shadows of Tomorrow' (1935) warned of the general decay which awaited Europe.

*1940 - 1945*

The Second World War did not spare the Netherlands.
Within five days the country was overrun (10-15 May 1940).
The most dramatic events during these days were the fights
with German paratroopers behind the westward moving
front and the destruction by firebombs of the centre of
Rotterdam. Then followed the occupation. The Dutch
Government, with Queen Wilhelmina and her family, were
evacuated to England, while the Dutch navy and merchant
navy sided with the Allies for the rest of the war.
The Netherlands received a special National Socialist
treatment. Racial similarity prompted the hope that the
Teutonic Dutch would be malleable to National Socialist
ideology. The country received a civilian administration
under the Austrian Nazi A.Seyss Inquart. Dutch
prisoners-of-war were set free by a special 'generous'
decision by Hitler himself. But German attempts to get a
great majority of the Dutch population on the National
Socialist side failed. The bombing of the unprotected
centre of Rotterdam had stirred up bad blood. Any
relationship between an occupying power and the
occupied is bound to be uneasy and unpleasant. Moreover,

the Germans needed the Netherlands not only as a strategically important link but also as a source of supplies, from which materials and later manpower had to be seized. It is never easy for a victor to win the hearts of the conquered.

The military defeat of the Netherlands left a deep imprint on the memory of the people even before the German forces started to be more ruthless, and certain measures against the Jews in particular showed that the occupation of the country was not just of military and strategical importance. The disillusion of the unjust attack of the Germans and the quick defeat of the Dutch was at first projected into bitter hatred for those Dutchmen who welcomed the Nazis and were prepared to use German help to obtain power. The old NSB, which just before the war had dwindled into a small party supported by 3 per cent of Dutch voters only, became the target of a great deal of Dutch resentment and disillusion. In their turn, the Dutch National Socialists became more aggressive and clung with greater zest to German protection. As a party it never succeeded in capturing more than 15 per cent of the Dutch population during the peak days of German victories (1940 - 1941). Soon this Dutch National Socialism became nothing more than an extension of German National Socialism, even though the leader of the Dutch movement (A.A.Mussert) imagined he still had an independent controlling position.

But within a few months it became clear that the Germans really wanted more than just loyal co-operation in military and economic matters. Gradually German pressure increased with the aim of subjecting the Dutch people into a position of involuntary collaboration and acceptance of Nazi ideology. In the course of two years Dutch administration was controlled by the Nazis by way of dismissal and appointment, with only a sprinkling of Dutch officials remaining out of fear and conviction that they were preventing worse conditions by staying in their places. Censorship, curbing of political life and terror did the rest of the work. The methods adopted by the German police and secret service in the Netherlands were for Western Europe particularly intensive, with more victims than in the rest of Western Europe. To a great extent this can be explained by the unfamiliarity of the Netherlands with the consequences of war and occupation in general. The Dutch state had been well-organized and orderly, most of the people did not see the necessity for sabotage and passive resistance to at least slow down measures and directives which came from the Germans. Up till 1943 the Dutch administrative system worked as well as ever. On the other hand, a great deal of naïveté and ingenuousness about the possibilities of German ruthless repression led to public mass demonstrations and general strikes which were repressed by the Nazis in a way surpassing the imagination of those who had dared to take part in such actions.

The application of the Nazi doctrine of anti-semitism was, in its consequences the most extreme. The Jews in the Netherlands were systematically isolated at first, later deported and finally destroyed. Of the 140,000 Jews living in the Netherlands before 1940, most of them for many generations, 104,000 were murdered (80 per cent). About 12,000 saved themselves by hiding or other means, 8,000 thanks to their marriage to a gentile - a so-called mixed marriage. Only 6,000 Jews returned from the German concentration camps. Especially for Amsterdam this massacre was a deep loss, the lively and interesting Jewish quarter was a dead corner of the city after the war. Sad also was the fact that the Dutch resistance only developed into a force of some significance when the deportations had been well under way, from July 1942, and could not do much at such a late date. Only a small minority of the Dutch people was individually prepared to take the severe risks of helping the Jews to hide.

But soon the rest of the Dutch population was to undergo the terror and arbitrariness of the German occupation. With the help of concentration camps, never before known in the Netherlands, 23,000 people died from brutality, murder, starvation and disease. Another symptom of the outlawry of the Dutch citizens was the Nazi-organized 'razzia', mass man-hunts carried out in cities and villages, first on Jews, later on able-bodied men to provide manpower for industry and defence works for the German war effort. By more normal means, through call-ups of employment agencies and personal summons, more and more men were also sent to work in Germany. Industry in the Netherlands was likewise forced to co-operate. To some extent, by sabotage, go-slow tactics and open refusal, by 'going underground' (hiding), the actual value of this forced labour was lessened. It will never be known how much these tactics helped.

The feelings towards the Germans turned to increasingly grim hatred from 1943 in particular. Dissatisfaction over the meagre rations, over the treatment of the forced labourers in Germany, the growing fear of the German terror and the rising hopes of an allied victory were the opportunistic motives for these anti-German sentiments. Pity for the victims of the Germans, anger at the lawlessness and misdeeds, at the violation of all values which the Dutch people had learned to treasure, were the more positive reasons for the changed attitude.

Three great demonstrative brave protests (at the time completely unknown in the rest of Europe) gave expression to the current mood. Almost the whole working class of Amsterdam went on strike in February 1941 as an open protest against mass arrests of Jews in the Jewish quarter. At this time, an allied victory seemed far away and the reason for the strike was purely humanitarian: pity for the Jewish victims gave this strike the character of human greatness. The initiative came from communist workers, the illegal Communist Party becoming the main organizing power of the strike, but the thousands who followed and who in turn stimulated others were of every creed and belonged to every political party. The strike first took the Nazis by surprise, but then they reacted fiercely with killings and arrests. The May strikes of 1943, pretty general in the whole country, with a concentrated force in industrial Twente and the farming areas in Friesland, were a protest against the radical measures the German occupying authorities had taken to suppress resistance by calling back the prisoners-of-war into camps. To stop this strike, the invader had again recourse to firing-squads, summary justice and mass-arrests, before 'order' was restored. The general railway strike began in September 1944, intended as an aid to the Allied War Effort. This time the strike was fully organized and the Dutch Government in London had directed it. The Allies had, since the invasion of France, reached the borders of the Netherlands. The strike continued until liberation which came much later than expected, paralysing nearly all railway traffic. The Resistance forces were able to support the railway personnel that had to go into hiding.

While the great majority of the Dutch people boiled up a few times only in a general open demonstration, protest was actively carried on by a relatively small minority in the Resistance, the 'underground' movement ('de ondergrondse'). At first only a few individuals spontaneously wrote and stencilled resistance letters and the illegal press soon developed, but gradually a greater number of young and old started to devote time and energy to a series of activities, despite the great risks of a vigourously reacting enemy (from ten to a maximum of a hundred thousand). In the course of the years 1942 and 1943 the organization became more effective and sophisticated. Help was extended to victims of the German terror: the Jews, the fleeing workers from Germany, and those who had to go into hiding; they had to be provided with food and the necessary forged documents. Then raiding groups were formed to attack the enemy, liberate prisoners, enter distribution centres and town halls in order to seize rationing coupons and documents. They carried out espionage, maintained contacts with Great Britain, built up an escape route to Switzerland and Spain or Scandinavia and helped refugees over the border. For the general public the successful distribution of illegal newspapers and pamphlets was of the greatest importance. And finally there was the illegal military training in preparation for the liberation, training in the handling of weapons, etc.

In the last year of the war, following the liberation of France, military operations began to affect the Netherlands gravely. In September 1944 the Allies broke through at Eindhoven, landed near Arnhem and Nijmegen and attempted with one stroke to cross the rivers Meuse, Waal and Rhine and form a continuous bridgehead. The battle of Arnhem (17-27 September) failed, thus affecting the whole plan. Only the province of North Brabant and large areas of Limburg were liberated and had to suffer as front line areas for the following seven months. In order to gain access to Antwerp via the Scheldt, the dykes of Walcheren were bombed by allied bombers, flooding the whole island. In the west of the Netherlands, the provinces of Holland, there followed a terrible winter of starvation for the population: as a revenge for the railway strike, transports of food from the east of the country to the west were deliberately stopped by the Nazis. Mercifully, the plan of some of the leading German authorities to flood Holland was confined to the destruction of the great Wieringermeerpolder. The liberation of the Netherlands in April and May 1945 brought an end to the terror of German occupation.

*'Verwoeste Stad' (destroyed city).*
*War monument by Zadkine in Rotterdam*

*1942 - 1963*

The actual attack of the Japanese forces on the
Netherlands East Indies began in January 1942. The fall of
Singapore (15 February 1942) decided the fate of the Dutch
colonies. A heroic stand by the Dutch navy in the Battle of
the Java Sea (27 February) could do nothing to prevent a
Japanese invasion. The Dutch colonial army in Java
capitulated on 9 March.
Very soon the European colonial minority was imprisoned
in large camps. The whole colonial administration was
taken over by the invader, and there began a period of
suffering, humiliation, brutalization and starvation for the
Europeans. Even harder to bear was the fact that families
were broken up, with many prisoners-of-war sent to Burma
and Japan for hard forced labour. Of the 80,000 internees
about 22,000 lost their lives.
The Allied victory over Japan, though long awaited, came
rather unexpectedly, certainly for the Dutch Government
which had little knowledge of events in the Far East. Plans
drawn up by high functionaries of the former colonial
administration while in exile in Australia or in internment
were crossed by the unexpected results of the capitulation

of Japan on 15 August 1945. On 17 August a group of Indonesian nationalists proclaimed the East Indian Archipelago an independent state - the Republic of Indonesia. It was difficult for the returning colonial administration, led by the Governor General Lieutenant H.J. van Mook (1894 - 1965), to negotiate with these nationalists, some of whose leaders had collaborated with the Japanese occupation authorities, for example Sukarno and Hatta. From the beginning, tension existed between the fiery nationalists and the indignant Dutch, which was heightened by the fact that the troops disarming and replacing the Japanese were at first not Dutch, but British. Dutch troops only arrived in October 1945. The British commander recognized the nationalists as partners for consultation and gave scant attention to the Dutch idea that Netherlands authority should be restored first.

As a consequence of this confusing situation, the new nationalist government had the opportunity to spread its authority all over Java. Armed groups were formed, equipped with captured Japanese weapons, which gradually gained the sympathetic support of the Javanese population. Japanese anti-western propaganda during the occupation had helped to make Indonesian public opinion increasingly anti-Dutch. The Europeans had 'lost face' when they proved powerless against the Japanese. Indonesian passions of hate and fury which had probably piled up during Japanese occupation, broke loose at the end of September in the form of lynching and killing. The unfortunate European internees, freed from their Japanese warders after Japan's capitulation, but still kept in their camps, were the main victims of this 'bersiap' period (October-December 1945). As a result, the small Indonesian nationalist group of intellectuals who had proclaimed the Republic were in a strong bargaining position, and the Netherlands Government finally decided to negotiate about the terms of Indonesia's future.

Negotiations proceeded over four years, sometimes seemingly successful, at other times completely at a standstill. Agreements drawn up to end what was in effect a state of war were signed but not implemented: distrust on both sides increased. The Dutch negotiators became convinced that no agreement with the nationalists could be relied upon, partly because of the latter's complete lack of control over the guerrilla bands.

In the Netherlands itself a fierce argument for and against the Javanese rising developed. The left-progressive view that every nation had the right to freely decide its destiny and that colonial days were over, went against the opinion of the centre and right-wing parties, whose view was that no single nation had the right to make a mess of his own country, and that in any case the Indonesians were not yet ready for full self-government. The debaters accused each other on the one hand with narrow-mindedness, gross self-interest and lack of any understanding of nationalism, on the other with empty idealism, ignorance and self-centred pedantry. The Netherlands Government was in great difficulties, because on the one side Van Mook took inspired measures on his own, trying to get the Dutch Government in tow, while on the other side Dutch divisions within the parties and groups made decisive action in any direction extremely problematic. Finally Van Mook set his mind on a federation (the Conference of Malino, 16-24 July 1946), whereby alongside the Republic of Java, the other islands of Sumatra, Celebes, Borneo and the Moluccas would be states with equal status. The Dutch Government accepted these ideas, and negotiations on this basis were carried on with the Republican nationalists.

In the end the Netherlands Government, however, lost patience. Two 'police-actions' were carried out in an attempt to force the situation in Java in favour of the federal plan. Both military operations (21 July-5 August 1947 and 19-24 December 1948) aroused international protest to an extent that could not be ignored despite easy military successes. In the UNO Security Council the USA and Australia protested and were supported by the Soviet Union and Great Britain. As a result of this international interference, commissions for negotiation and mediation were sent to Indonesia to open discussion again and in particular to force the Netherlands to make far-reaching concessions to the Republic. A Round Table Conference in The Hague (August-November 1949) ended with the handing over of sovereignty by the Netherlands to the United States of Indonesia (27 December 1949), of which the Indonesian Republic would be one of the member states. The Dutch Parliament accepted the results of this Conference with the necessary majority, but with the inclusion of several clauses which guaranteed the independence of all peoples within the USI and insisted explicitly on the federal character of this partnership. In this way the other states, which had more sympathy for the Netherlands and were prepared to co-operate with the Dutch more closely, had a chance to develop. A further clause referred to Western New Guinea, which was temporarily to remain under Dutch control.

If there were politicians who expected that, as a result of independence, relations between the Netherlands and Indonesia would improve, they were soon to be disappointed. In 1950 the Republican Government rescinded the federal constitution in favour of one Republic embracing the whole archipelago with a central government residing in Djakarta, the new name for Batavia. The right of self-determination, to which the Amboinese appealed after the abolition of the State of East Indonesia, was not honoured. Amboina's resistance was considered a rebellion and stamped out. Relations between the Netherlands and Indonesia worsened by this hasty abrogation of one of the crucial articles in the agreement of the Round Table Conference. In Indonesia, where a large Dutch minority still resided and where Dutch economic interests were widely spread throughout Indonesian public life, much of the unrest and confusion within the Republic was blamed on Dutch intrigues and attempts at neo-colonialism.

But the last bone of contention between the Dutch and Indonesians soon proved to be Western New Guinea, which was retained by the Netherlands in the treaty of the RTC waiting for a later specific understanding to be reached. The Dutch hoped that it would be possible to save this area gradually from the turmoil of Indonesian chaos and decline, and justified this hope by pointing out that racially the Papua inhabitants were fundamentally different from the other Indonesian peoples. To a certain extent Western New Guinea became for many Dutchmen a matter of prestige, and soon this *colony' was considered as a kind of model to prove to the whole world what western enlightenment could perform in a primitive land. Indonesia on the other hand always claimed Western New Guinea as an integral part of Indonesia and refused to negotiate about this area unless the Netherlands promised beforehand to accept the Indonesian point of view. Gradually Sukarno, the leading statesman and head of the State of Indonesia, built up his campaign for annexing Western New Guinea. All kinds of pressure were used to get the Netherlands to agree. In 1956 Indonesia denounced the Treaty with the Netherlands, in 1957 all Dutch enterprise in Indonesia was nationalized and all Dutch nationals still in Indonesia were expelled, in 1960 diplomatic relations were severed. Only when the Dutch Government realized that no international help or even moral support for their point of view was to be expected (the United States and Australia for example made this very clear), was Western New Guinea (Irian) finally handed over to Indonesia, under a UNO guarantee that the Papuan population would have the freedom to decide their own future before 1969. On the 1st of May, 1963, New Guinea changed hands. A kind of plebiscite in 1969 organized by Indonesia finally decided that this area would remain within Indonesia.

The Indonesian question had been a very heavy burden and had, after a protracted and difficult period of negotiations, military operations and rebellions, led to a total defeat for the Netherlands. All influence and all possible economic interests in Indonesia were severed. It had been indeed a painful and costly retreat. Only after 1966 did relations between both countries begin to improve.

*1945 - 1960*

The Netherlands encountered many other setbacks, but
generally speaking, except for the failure of the Indonesian
policy, other events had a more favourable outcome.
The colonial problem of the Dutch West Indies at any rate
seemed to be solved in a peaceful and orderly way. A new
relationship was entered into with Surinam and the Antilles
in an atmosphere of friendliness: within a new Union both
areas would have their own separate governments and be
considered on an equal footing with the Netherlands in that
Union (15 December 1954). This, of course, did not solve
the growing internal economic and social problems of
these Caribbean and Latin American communities. Both
had experienced a considerable boom during the war, but
gradually after the war old and new economic problems
arose. In the Antilles, where Curaçao had become an
important centre for refineries of Venezuelan oil,
mechanization of the plants and the increasing threat that
Venezuelan refineries would take over created difficulties.
More and more jobs were lost by the negro population and
in May 1969 a general strike developed into a riot in which
parts of the city of Willemstad were burned down. In

Surinam, bauxite was less in demand than it had been during the war, and the economic problems of this racially very divided country worsened.

More important for the Netherlands themselves were the problems in Europe. Already during the war, the basis had been laid for closer co-operation with Belgium and Luxemburg, but 'Benelux' did not lead to the expected complete economic union and was to be overshadowed by greater and wider combinations in which these countries took part. However, at an early period after 1945 it was an example of what could be done to break away from the old-fashioned parochial autonomy of each separate state. A customs union was formed on 15 July 1949. In a wider field the Netherlands worked along with the various plans for European integration, for example the European Payments Union, the European Council and the European Coal and Steel Community. All these steps finally led to the creating of the European Economic Community in 1957, in which the Netherlands became one of the six members together with West Germany, Italy, France, Belgium and Luxemburg (Great Britain joined in 1971). Within the Community, several agreements on matters of common economic interests and integration, with important consequences for internal affairs, were reached. The great stumbling-block proved to be the agrarian problem, whilst the Netherlands were rather unhappy that no counterweight could be found against the strong influence of France as long as West Germany accepted French leadership. From the very beginning the Dutch representatives in the Community championed the entrance of Great Britain into the Common Market of the Community, which in 1971 was made possible at last. Of even more direct practical consequence was the decision to definitely end the earlier Dutch attitude of neutrality towards the main European political and military problems. It was realized that a small country could not remain aloof from international power politics and in fact seemed to invite an aggressor by its own military weakness. The aggressive policy of Soviet Russia, begun in 1944 in Poland and alarmingly intensified in the ensuing years with the coup d'état in Prague in 1948, the Blockade of Berlin in 1948-9, the attack on South Korea in 1950, forced the Netherlands Government to adopt a realistic policy, and on 14 April 1949 the Netherlands signed the North Atlantic Pact and did the utmost to co-operate with the creation of a European army, which resulted in the formation of the Nato forces in 1955.

Internal politics did not change appreciably. The party system was barely altered, although at first many attempts at renovation were made. Much was expected from the SDAP's change into a Labour Party (called 'Partij van de Arbeid'), incorporating the left-wing liberals. Although still clinging to the hope of a future socialist state, the party intended to lose its typical working-class character by attracting as many people from the middle classes as possible. Basically unconfessional in set-up, the party was to cater for enrolling Catholics and Protestants in great numbers by explicitly shedding any indication of atheism or anti-clericalism. The two-pronged attempt at a 'break-through' by this new Labour Party was unsuccessful and any hope of a two- or three-party system after the British example faded. Although the 'Partij van de Arbeid' received the support of a greater number of intellectuals, the majority of voters from the middle classes remained loyal to their old liberal and confessional parties. Catholics and Protestants also remained loyal to their parties. In the 1946 elections the Labour Party fell far short of the expected majority of more than 50 seats (it only won 29); the Catholics obtained 32 seats and, to the surprise of everyone, the Protestants held their 23 seats. It cannot be denied that the existing party system had received a new lease of life: the liberals recovered from their all but desperate position before 1940, the Catholics called their party a People's Party instead of 'State Party', and the Communists won more seats (10) than ever before or after. But the greatest internal changes of the country were not to be found in political life. A definite structural change in society was achieved, more important than any change in party names or adoption of splendid party programs, exemplified in the new combination of parties that took upon itself the responsibility of government. The Socialists and Catholics co-operated to form a 'pink-tinted' government, and with no transient economic crisis to contend with, brought about a very close intermingling of state and society. A more positively directed ideal of a social community was fostered, in which the less well-off would receive support and protection from the State. It was discovered that only by intensive state interference could threatening economic depressions and unemployment be warded off. A change in tax policy, social legislation, and deliberate economic interference were steps intentionally taken: a measure of social levelling was aimed at in a socio-capitalistic structure.

After the liberation, the general situation in the Netherlands had sunk to an alarmingly low level. Enormous state debts, great war damage, a worn-out, underfed population, a housing backlag of 5 years, gigantic losses in Indonesia and the temporary falling away of the economic German hinterland, all helped to crush the country. As compared with West Germany, whose economic recovery in the 1950s would be equally 'miraculous', the Netherlands had not suffered destruction like most German cities, but on the other hand the Dutch had to rebuild economic life with two serious additional setbacks: the necessity of immediate rearmament (which West Germany was forbidden before 1955) and the burden of the Indonesian question which meant practically the waging of a minor overseas war up till 1949. The greatest intitial handicap was the deficit in the trading balance and the unfavourable dollar situation as its consequence. As a result, the acquirement of machinery, building material, coal and other essential raw materials was seriously hampered.

Three factors made the Netherlands economic recovery possible. First, the Government showed great determination in taking measures to deal with economic life, such as wage and price control, strict control on currency, and a radical monetary purge. The rigorous policy of taxation carried out by the very able Minister of Finance, P.Lieftinck (b. 1902) who remained in office until 1952, gave the Dutch Government indispensible financial strength. In the second place, social peace was a very important aid to industrialization and production. Though a Communist Labour Union set up in 1945 attempted to cause unrest by strike actions, the other trade unions, among them the largest socialist National Workers Union, did all they could to preserve peace among the workers. A Labour Council, in which workers, employers and the government were represented, maintained close contact and played an important role in establishing and keeping labour peace. Thirdly, the Marshall Plan (1947) helped the Netherlands over an extremely dangerous period of dollar shortage. By this European Recovery Program, the Netherlands received the huge sum of 978 million dollars (of which 133 in loans) over four years, under the acceptable conditions of economic European reconstruction and integration.

From 1948 conditions began to develop more favourably. Symbolic of this change of time was the decision in that same year by Queen Wilhelmina to abdicate in favour of her daughter Juliana. The Queen, who had reigned for more than 50 years, handed over the heavy task when the greatest difficulties had been overcome and a new epoch could be considered to be beginning.

The trading deficit - still 1.7 billion guilders in 1947 - fell to 222 million in 1949, and in 1951 balance was achieved. Industrial production, although costs had risen also, surpassed by 44 per cent in 1953 the level reached in 1938. International conditions also helped: international trade was freed as far as was possible, and the economic advantages of Benelux began to be felt. Germany recovered quickly, agreements with Indonesia (1949) brought some relief and the standard of living started to rise. Increasing prosperity permitted relaxation of some restrictions: an end was made to food rationing in 1949, wages were increased in 1954 for the first time because of the favourable economic situation, taxes were lowered slightly and the social services extended in a spectacular way (e.g. free education on the elementary level, old age pensions, unemployment insurance, etc.). This restoration of prosperity and economic stability was all the more striking when seen against new setbacks. The cost of living rose and some inflationary tendencies began to worry the economic advisers of the Government. The end of Marshall Plan help and the Korean war rocked the economic stability for a while. The flood disaster of February 1953 caused great hardship in South Holland and Zeeland. But though all these setbacks slowed down the rapid economic growth, they could not stop it.

Of course not all problems were solved by economic recovery and socio-capitalistic structural changes. It was realized that the Dutch economic situation was after all partly dependent on international movements and especially vulnerable because of its lack of raw materials and its great share in economic services (shipping, aviation, banking, insurance, etc.). An additional problem became the rapid increase in population concentrated in a relatively small part of the country (Holland). This increase was first caused by the longer life-expectancy, which was about 70 years as against 44 in 1900. But after a slowing-down in the 1950s compared with the post-war peak, the birthrate also rose rapidly. In 1920 the population was almost 7 million, in 1938 it had increased to 8 million and in 1953 to 10,5. Population density was in 1960 an average of 344 inhabitants per square kilometer, one of the highest rates in the world. The Government became more and more worried about the problem of full employment in the future. Propaganda for birth control met with strong objections from Protestants and Catholics on religious grounds, and the only solution appeared to be the encouragement of emigration. Up till the 1960s many young Dutchmen emigrated with their families to countries like Canada and Australia with governmental help and subsidies. One of the main problems of this increase in population proved to be the never-ending housing shortage. The original shortage after 1945 could be explained by war destruction and stoppage of building, but soon the increasing population added to this problem, and with the rise of prosperity people's demands for good accommodation maximized the need for new houses instead of old dwellings and particularly those in slum areas.

Perhaps the many problems and worries the Netherlands had to live with, in spite of rapid economic recovery, were best reflected in the creative arts. In an unprecedented and, internationally, exceptional way, the Dutch socio-capitalistic state supported and stimulated art by subsidizing cultural societies and unions and commissioning individual artists. While new buildings, out of the sheer need for speed, tended to be over-simple and unimaginative, often monotonous and dull, the applied arts were used to ornament wherever possible, but naturally the artists were left free to express themselves in their own way.

The first 'generation' of Dutch artists after the war still lived under the indelible shadow of the sad years of economic depression and war. The many war monuments erected after 1945 gave the opportunity to many sculptors to express their grim memories in a most 'monumental' and realistic way. Here the monuments of Mari Andriessen (b. 1897) and John Rädecker (1885 - 1957) should be mentioned. In literature, many authors felt the need to liberate themselves from their own frustrating memories by writing about them in a highly sophisticated and Freudian way. Simon Vestdijk (1898 - 1971), well-known already before the war, went on to write his many novels, of which a great number were based on childhood memories. G.K.van het Reve (b. 1923), tried to rid himself of his personal worries by describing in clever autobiographical prose the nightmare of youth and adolescence. Perhaps the greatest writer of post-war Dutch literature is Willem Frederik Hermans (b. 1921) who based his imaginative writing on the perennial problem of human misunderstanding, often with the events of war occupation as a background.

In the 1950s, other artists tried more intentionally to break away from more easily understandable, realistic and traditional forms of expression, although Hermans could be surrealistic if he needed to. The Cobra group of painters and poets tried to scream and stammer their protests and non-conformism. The paintings of Karel Appel (b. 1921) were wilfully barbaric in colour and shape, just as the surrealistic poems of Lucebert (b. 1924) were intentionally associative and primarily emotive. Dadaism, abstract art, even pop-art, but in that case avant-la-lettre and whatever name one likes to give to these works of art, seemed to break loose. Paradoxically these artists hoped to come closer to a greater public by their attempts at direct simplicity and naïve intuition, and instead often got bogged down in hyperbolic individualism which was certainly not appreciated by the common man. It was perhaps a prophetic movement, expressing beforehand a mentality which responded to the needs of the young in the 1960s rather than those of the more soberminded and hard-working generation of the 1950s.

Indeed, a serious and enthusiastic drive for economic growth still governed the recovering Netherlands during the 1950s. Almost symbolic of this was the way the nation reacted to the flood disaster of 1953: first a wave of communal feeling swept the country, and when the necessary help had been given and the dykes repaired, the next problem was ready to be tackled. Although it will take years to complete, a better dyke system will, in the near future, protect South Holland and Zeeland more efficiently than in 1953. The so-called 'Delta Plan' (accepted by Parliament in 1957) envisaged the closing of the great river mouths with a series of massive and long dykes, sluices and bridges built along the seacoast of the South Holland and Zeeland islands.

*Part of the 'Deltaplan'*

# 31          The burden of prosperity

*from 1960 onwards*

In the 1960s, the Netherlands stood on the threshold of
happy times. The terrible problem of West New Guinea was
'solved' by the great powers in 1963. After the Cuba crisis
in 1962, the threat of international conflict and a Third
World War began to recede. The Netherlands passed
through a stage of unprecedented prosperity and
previously unknown economic growth. Rotterdam
developed into the greatest port in the world, its gigantic
lay-out of harbours and factory sites, based on
'Europort'-plans, started to function from 1960 onwards. In
1960, the greatest find of natural gas near Slochteren
(Groningen) suddenly gave the Netherlands its own
adequate source of energy for decades to come. More than
at any other time the Dutch could indeed use the slogan:
'You never had it so good.'
But somehow those happy times did not come about.
Instead, the period was to be wrought by unrest, discontent
and tension. Why?
Paradoxically, prosperity made over-population almost
unbearable. The rising standard of living required better
accommodation, the housing shortage was felt all the more

painfully. Everybody longed for his own car and traffic congestion became a major irritant. In 1959, with a population of 11.4 million, 450,000 cars were in use; in 1969, with a population of 13 million, 2,290,000 cars were on the roads. The most densely populated areas began to exchange their last green woods and pastures for asphalt plains of roads, intersections, and big blocks of flats: 'the slums of tomorrow'. Noise prevailed over birdsong and the chattering of many, many children. The increasing number of old people began to feel very lonely indeed in the ever growing masses.

How could this over-population be overcome? Encouragement of emigration continued, but with less success than before. Attempts at encouraging people to move to less populated parts of the country did not help, although the Government set an example by removing several departmental offices out of The Hague to cities like Groningen and Maastricht. In the long run, birth control would be more effective; from 1960 most political parties and denominations began to accept the need for it, in spite of the directives from the Vatican. The 'pill' came into almost general use and had a tangible effect on the birth-rate. The decline of the birth-rate is at this moment somewhat hidden by the fact that young people tend to marry and have children at an earlier age than they did before 1960, but the results will certainly be noticeable in twenty or thirty years.

Economic growth also created its own problems: pollution is of course the most drastic attending consequence. The great river Rhine began to be poisoned by industrial waste, the air above Europort became polluted with smog, the noise of aircraft near modern Schiphol became intolerable. Many branches of industry could not keep up with the speed of change and growth, others suffered from competition within the Common Market. The labour-absorbing textile industry was hit by rising wages and foreign competition. Mining in South Limburg became less profitable, necessitating a switch to the chemical industry - most collieries closed down. Agriculture in general suffered severely from Common Market competition and soon proved to be over-employed and too much split up into small private parcels of land.

Rationalization, mechanization, labour redundancy and the liquidation of small farms, all this caused dismay and discontent. Many small factories and family firms had to amalgamate or go bankrupt.

Economic growth also appeared to create inflation. Prices and wages became one of the greatest worries for all the cabinets after 1958. Over-employment and high wages forced employers to look for the cheap labour of unskilled workers elsewhere. Foreign labourers were encouraged to come: first from Italy and Spain, later from Turkey and North Africa. In 1969, more than 100,000 foreign workers had labour permits in the Netherlands. In the over-populated West, these newcomers caused further housing problems and often racial tension as well.

Prosperity improved the means of cummunication and stimulated mobility. Every Dutch family owned a TV, and the majority became accustomed to a holiday abroad. The advantage was that the world entered the Dutch household. The problems of the United States, of desegregation first, of the war in Vietnam later, could be followed by every Dutchman and many of them formed an opinion about it. Rebelliousness elsewhere, like the revolt in Paris of May 1968, stimulated and inspired Dutch students. The Second Vatican Council was eagerly followed by Dutch Catholics (1962-3). Sympathy with the under-developed countries overseas created a sense of duty to help.

No party, from 1963 onwards, dared leave out of its program a paragraph about aid for developing countries and no government dared to save money by abandoning the principle that at least 1 per cent of the national income should be spent on development in needy countries - a decision unprecedented in the world. On the other hand, this openness towards the world created a sense of constant imperfection, of restless criticism shifting from one target to another.

Another factor which explains the discontent and restlessness in the Netherlands was the estrangement between the bureaucratic system of administration and the citizens, between the experts and the laymen, between the 'establishment' and those who were 'out'. The new socio-capitalistic system required a great deal of sophisticated expertise and a rapid expansion of state administrative activity. The increasing interference and the apparent growth of power created distrust in the citizens, who felt like pawns on a chessboard. Postponement of decisions stimulated criticism of snail-like evasion of responsibility, the taking of quick decisions caused the feeling that bureaucracy was authoritarian.

Prosperity also caused quite a rapid and sudden change of mentality. A different attitude towards work as a burden rather than a fulfilment of life seemed to penetrate into many minds. Young people tended to change work rapidly and could easily do so because of over-employment. The rise in the standard of living increased demands rather than a sense of fulfilment. The young were quicker to adapt to the new circumstances than the old, and the generation gap became more clear-cut than ever before. The older generation was still afraid of unemployment and economic crisis, the young took prosperity for granted and were only irritated when they discovered that many groups within the nation had missed the bus and remained in the backwaters of poverty or at least neglect. The older generation feared any repetition of an attack by a foreign enemy and wanted to be better prepared to ward off such an attack than had been possible in Hitler's time, the young were optimistic pacifists and again pleaded one-sided disarmament. The older generation looked cynically at all that seemed new and promising, the young shifted their admiration from one model Utopia to another: from Ghana to China, from China to Cuba, from Cuba to Chili. The old looked up to the former and present American allies, the young blamed the United States for its war in Vietnam.

All these tensions and problems of a prosperous Netherlands found expression in many demonstrations and acts of protest. In the capital city of Amsterdam in particular, unrest became pretty well endemic. As early as 1965, the movement of the Provos became world-famous, comparable at the time with the students protest in Berkeley, California. In their odd behaviour which was wilfully asocial and directed against all the customs and habits of the average 'bourgeois', they tried to 'provoke' society and were at least successful in clashing with the Amsterdam police. The wedding-ceremony of Crown Princess Beatrix to a German commoner who had served for a few months in the German army at the end of World War II was seriously disturbed by the Provos and their followers (10 March 1966), and a real revolution seemed imminent when striking labourers temporarily joined forces with Provos and students in severe attacks on the police and a newspaper building in Amsterdam (14-15 June 1966). Many universities had student revolts in the course of 1968-9, following the Paris example. In May 1969 some university buildings were temporarily occupied by students, and the Minister of Education hastily had a law of university administrative reform passed by Parliament, by which students and administrative staff had equal responsibility with the teaching staff in almost all university decisions, a form of legislation which in its progressiveness was equalled only by some revolutionary universities in Germany (1971).

But even these spectacular and noisy external symptoms of unrest and discontent have had perhaps less consequence and influence than expected. In political life, except for a great deal of anxiety among many authorities, things developed much less dramatically, and change was relatively slight. The only party that really suffered in the 1960s was the Roman Catholic People's Party (KVP), which in the end had lost nearly one third of its support in the elections. All other parties held most of their votes, in spite of many inner conflicts, clashes and splits, and despite the sometimes severe competition of several successive new parties which succeeded for a while in capturing the floating vote. With one interruption of only two years, the confessional parties together with the (conservative) liberals were able to remain in power and take governmental responsibility from 1958 onwards. It is an open question, moreover, whether a left-centre government could have done most things differently from what these right-centre governments had been forced to do.

Other developments should be mentioned here which were much more dramatic and will have greater consequences than the external unrest that caught the eye. Perhaps one can speak of three major 'revolutions'.

The first one could be called the 'sexual revolution'. In a country where traditional Puritanism and conservative Catholicism had been coloured by the Victorianism of the leading bourgeoisie, this revolution came as a shock. It started in the early 1960s with the acceptance of birthcontrol by nearly all parties and denominations and an open and general discussion on the benefits of the use of the pill; it was soon followed by an explicit toleration of pre-marital intercourse, homosexuality and sex-education in the schools (1965-6), to end with violent discussions on whether abortion and the necessary clinical provisions for it should be allowed. It is improbable that within the forseeable future the Dutch could ever return to the traditional pre-1960 sexual morality.

The second revolution took place in education. The main legislation in this respect called for a complete renewal of the secondary schools (for children between 12 and 18 years). A wider choice of subjects was made possible with an easier transfer from one type of school to another. It meant in fact the definite though tardy end of the traditional humanistic-classical education in which Latin and even Greek had been the main compulsory subjects, and introduced a system more in common with Anglo-Saxon examples (1963). In the near future, new legislation will change the organization of the university, making it a training system for professional purposes whilst research will probably be hived off to separate institutions. The other important change in education is another consequence of prosperity. More and more children stay at school for a longer period and to the highest possible level. A tendency towards intellectual work will decrease the supply of skilled physical labour in the labour market, with all the problems connected with such a development.

The third revolution is the complete change in outlook and attitude of the Roman Catholics in the Netherlands. From 1960 onwards, this large section of the population (40 per cent) suddenly changed face: formerly counted amongst the most loyal adherents of Rome and the most pious and conservative believers in the world, they became one of the most rebellious, progressive and modernistic groups in religious and ecclesiastical matters. Similar tendencies were discernible in the Protestants, but they were never as dramatic and sudden - the Protestants had already started emancipation in the second half of the 19th century and had never shown the kind of coherence and discipline the

Dutch Catholics had maintained throughout the years. To a certain extent it was proof of the real intellectual emancipation which the Dutch Catholics had at last found. Up till 1960, their discipline and conservatism in religious matters had been a sign of defensive 'sticking together' against the angry outer world. Now they could afford to become independent and self-confident. In the late 1950s warnings of the 'wind of change' had been clear. In particular the number of calls to convent life, always very high in the Netherlands, decreased and never revived. The Second Vatican Council (1962-3) created among Dutch Catholics great expectations and radicalized their ideas most rapidly. Dutch Catholics expected from the Council that new roads would be opened up for oecumenical co-operation with all other Christian Churches, and demands for abolition of the celibacy of the priesthood and acceptance of the contraceptive pill were voiced. And when all this did not come off as easily as expected, the Dutch Catholics lost respect for Rome. The high clergy, under the leadership of the Archbishop of Utrecht, tried to ride the inner storms by quickly renouncing all their earlier pronouncements and taking the lead in reform within the Dutch church community.

The success of the Catholic revolution became apparent by what has been called the process of 'deconfessionalization'. The typical separateness of all Catholic organization began to crumble. This did not mean that these organizations vanished, and it is quite possible that many of them will regain their old position in the end, but within them a sudden willingness was shown to co-operate with non-Catholics and many individual Catholics suddenly no longer seemed to bother about their membership, and were prepared, if need be, to enter other Protestant or non-denominational organizations. The bishops also withheld their usual advice. The Catholic People's Party in particular had to suffer the consequences of this deconfessionalization, as, until well into the 1960s, it had been the party with the largest support. Within three elections this support declined: at the elections of 1963 the KVP still held 31 per cent of the total vote, in 1967 it went down to 26.5 per cent and in 1971 it did not hold more than 21.9 per cent. It seems improbable that the party

will ever succeed in recovering these losses.
Perhaps one can say that the period after 1960 was one of
unrest and change, and to a certain extent of 'unhappy
times'. But the Dutch scene has indeed been not merely
prosperous and purely materialistic, but highly emotional,
tense and sensationally changeable. Since 1960 the Dutch
people have not known one dull moment in their lives.

*Riots on Dam Square. Amsterdam 1968*

# Genealogy

**1 House of Habsburg** (see chapters 8, 9, 10 and 11)

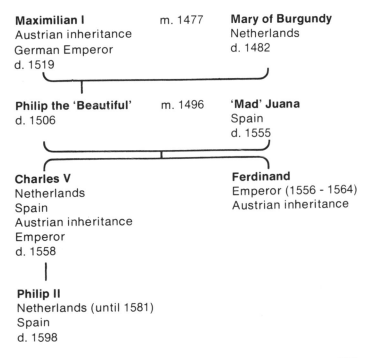

| | | |
|---|---|---|
| **Maximilian I**<br>Austrian inheritance<br>German Emperor<br>d. 1519 | m. 1477 | **Mary of Burgundy**<br>Netherlands<br>d. 1482 |
| **Philip the 'Beautiful'**<br>d. 1506 | m. 1496 | **'Mad' Juana**<br>Spain<br>d. 1555 |
| **Charles V**<br>Netherlands<br>Spain<br>Austrian inheritance<br>Emperor<br>d. 1558 | | **Ferdinand**<br>Emperor (1556 - 1564)<br>Austrian inheritance |
| **Philip II**<br>Netherlands (until 1581)<br>Spain<br>d. 1598 | | |

**II House of Orange-Nassau** (see chapters 28, 30 and 31)

**William the 'Rich' (Nassau)**               m. 1531
1487 - 1559

**William of Orange**          m. 1561          (2) **Anne of Saxe**
1533 - 1584                                      1544 - 1577
Stadth. 1560 - 1568
        1572 - 1584

        **Maurice**
        1567 - 1625
        Stadth. 1584 - 1625

                **Fred. Henry**     m. 1625     **Amalia of Solm**
                1584 - 1647                      1602 - 1675
                Stadth. 1625 - 1647

                        **William II**
                        1626 - 1650
                        Stadth. 1647 - 1650 ——

| | | | |
|---|---|---|---|
| John William Friso | 1687 - 1711 | | |
| William IV | 1711 - 1751 | Stadth. | 1747 - 175 |
| William V | 1748 - 1806 | Stadth. | 1751 - 179 |
| William I | 1772 - 1843 | King | 1813 - 184 |
| William II | 1792 - 1849 | King | 1840 - 184 |
| William III | 1817 - 1890 | King | 1849 - 189 |
| Wilhelmina | 1880 - 1962 | Queen | 1890 - 194 |
| Juliana | 1909 | Queen | 1948 |

Beatrix m. 1966 Claus of Amsberg         Irene m. 1964 Carel Hugo
1938              1926                    1939            1930

        William-Alexander 1967              Carlos 1970
        John Friso 1968
        Constantine 1969

**(2) Juliana of Stolberg**
1506 - 1580

. 1583    **(4) Louise de Coligny**    **John the Elder**
1555 - 1620    1535 - 1606

**Frisian Stadtholders**

m. 1641    **Maria Henrietta Stuart**
1631 - 1660

**William III**    m. 1677    **Mary Stuart**
1650 - 1702    1662 - 1695
Stadth. 1672 - 1702

| | | |
|---|---|---|
| m. 1709 | Marie Louise of Hessen-Kassel | 1688 - 1765 |
| m. 1734 | Anna of Hannover | 1709 - 1759 |
| m. 1767 | Wilhelmina of Prussia | 1751 - 1820 |
| m. 1791 | Wilhelmina Frederika of Prussia | 1774 - 1837 |
| m. 1816 | Anna Paulowna of Russia | 1795 - 1865 |
| m. 1879 | Emma of Waldeck Pyrmont | 1858 - 1934 |
| | Regentess | 1890 - 1898 |
| m. 1901 | Henry of Mecklenburg-Schwerin | 1876 - 1934 |
| m. 1937 | Bernard of Lippe Biesterfeld | 1911 |

rma    Margriet m. 1967 Peter of Vollenhoven    Christina
1943    1939    1947

Maurice 1968
Bernard 1969
Peter-Christian 1972

## Results of general elections held in the Netherlands since the introduction of general suffrage (in %)

| Parties | 1922 | 1925 | 1929 | 1933 | 1937 | 194 |
|---|---|---|---|---|---|---|
| Catholic | 29.9 | 28.6 | 29.6 | 27.9 | 28.8 | 30. |
| Anti-revolutionary | 13.7 | 12.2 | 11.6 | 13.4 | 16.4 | 12. |
| Christian-Historic. Un. | 10.9 | 9.9 | 10.5 | 9.1 | 7.5 | 7. |
| Orthodox Reformed | 0.9 | 2.0 | 2.3 | 2.5 | 1.9 | 2. |
| Orthodox Protestant | — | — | — | — | — | — |
| Liberal | 9.3 | 8.7 | 7.4 | 7.0 | 4.0 | 6. |
| Radical Liberal | 4.6 | 6.1 | 6.2 | 5.1 | 5.9 | — |
| Reformist Socialist (DS 70) | — | — | — | — | — | — |
| Social-Democrat | 19.4 | 22.9 | 23.9 | 21.5 | 22.0 | 28. |
| Pacifist Socialist | — | — | — | — | — | — |
| Communist | 1.8 | 1.2 | 2.0 | 3.2 | 3.3 | 10. |
| Other parties (getting enough votes to be represented in Parliament) | 2.5 | 3.6[1] | 3.2[1] | 5.4[1] | 4.2[2] | — |

[1] = mainly conservative farmers' parties
[2] = mainly National Socialist party (NSB)
[3] = Catholic conservative
[4] = three parties: progressive Catholic - 1,8, conservative farme
    conservative small holders' party - 1.5

| 948 | 1952 | 1956 | 1959 | 1963 | 1967 | 1971 | |
|---|---|---|---|---|---|---|---|
| .0 | 28.7 | 31.7 | 31.6 | 31.9 | 26.5 | 21.9 | Catholic |
| 3.2 | 11.3 | 9.9 | 9.4 | 8.7 | 9.9 | 8.6 | |
| 9.2 | 8.9 | 8.4 | 8.1 | 8.6 | 8.1 | 6.3 | Protestant |
| 2.4 | 2.4 | 2.3 | 2.2 | 2.3 | 2.0 | 2.4 | |
| — | — | — | — | — | 0.9 | 1.6 | |
| 3.0 | 8.8 | 8.8 | 12.2 | 10.3 | 10.7 | 10.6 | |
| — | — | — | — | 'D.66': | 4.4 | 6.8 | Liberal & |
| — | — | — | — | — | — | 5.3 | Radical |
| 5.6 | 32.7 | 30.3 | 30.3 | 28.0 | 23.5 | 24.6 | |
| — | — | — | 1.8 | 3.0 | 2.8 | 1.4 | Socialist & |
| 7.7 | 6.2 | 4.8 | 2.4 | 2.8 | 3.6 | 3.9 | Communist |
| .3[3] | 2.7[3] | — | — | 2.9[1] | 4.7[1] | 4.7[4] | Others |

⟶ party founded (with others)
by members coming from the
parties indicated

rty - 1.1,

# Suggestions for further reading

## General

P.J.Blok, **History of the people of the Netherlands.** 5 vols. New York/London, 1898 - 1912. An English translation of a Dutch standard work, thorough and extensive, but rather out of date. Most attention paid to political and economic, less to social and cultural aspects.

G.Edmundson, **History of Holland.** London, 1922. Reliable, mainly political history. Starts with Burgundian period. Concise.

B.H.M.Vlekke, **The evolution of the Dutch Nation.** New York, 1945. Best up-to-date work. Concise.

**Some special studies** (for the general reader)

*(Late) Middle Ages*

J.Huizinga, **The waning of the Middle Ages.** London, 1924. A study in the forms of life, thought and art in France and the Netherlands in the 14th and the 15th centuries. Reprinted in post-war paperbacks (i.e. Pelican). Classical Dutch work.

J.Huizinga, **Erasmus.** London/New York, 1924. Reprinted in post-war paperbacks. One of the best Dutch historical biographies.

*Republic (last half 16th, 17th & 18th centuries)*

P.Geyl, **The Revolt of the Netherlands (1555 - 1609).** London, 1932. **The Netherlands Divided (1600 - 1648).** London, 1936. Both books recently reprinted. Useful historical survey of the eighty years' war, stresses relations between the Northern Netherlands and the Dutch-speaking parts of present Belgium. Many theses and views of Geyl on Dutch history may be found in the form of lectures and essays in his **History of the Low Countries. Episodes and Problems.** London, 1964.

C.V.Wedgwood, **William the Silent (1533 - 1584).** London, 1944. Several reprints in paperback. A very good biography.
J.L.Motley, (amongst other works) **The Rise of the Dutch Republic.** 1860. This work, though well written and exciting to read, is obsolete by its old-fashioned idealization and romanticization of the Dutch rebels and the beginnings of the Republic.

C.H.Wilson, **The Dutch Republic and the civilization of the seventeenth century.** New York, 1968. Stresses Anglo- and Scottish-Dutch relations. Well illustrated.

J.Huizinga, **Dutch civilization in the seventeenth century & other essays.** New York, 1968. Title essay gives an excellent characteristic view of the Golden Age.

K.H.D.Haley, **The Dutch in the seventeenth century.** London, 1972. Concise survey with good choice of illustrations.

Charles R.Boxer, **The Dutch Seaborne Empire**

**(1600 - 1800).** New York, 1965. A lively and knowledgeable study not just on Dutch expansion but also on the background of the home country.

*Kingdom (19th & 20th centuries)*

A.van den Bosch, **Dutch foreign policy since 1815. A study in small powers' politics.** The Hague, 1959. A good introduction to this specialized subject.

W.Warmbrunn, **The Dutch and German occupation.** New York, 1963. One of the first serious surveys of the period 1940 - 1945.

J Goudsblom, **Dutch Society.** Random House (paperback), 1968. A sociological analysis of the contemporary scene.

**On history of the Dutch overseas**

B.H.M.Vlekke, **Nusantara - a history of the East Indian Archipelago.** New York, 1943 (reprinted after the war). A very good, clear and balanced book.

D.W.Davies, **A primer of Dutch seventeenth-century overseas trade.** The Hague, 1961. An introductory survey on all trade contacts within and without Europe.

W.F.Wertheim, **Indonesian society in transition.** The Hague/Bandung, 1956 (reprinted 1959). Analyses the economic and social changes in Indonesia since the second half of the 19th century, with special attention to indigenous society.

For more **specialized expert studies** it necessary to know Dutch; the following are recommended:
**Algemene Geschiedenis der Nederlanden.** Edited by J.A.van Houtte, J.F.Niermeyer, J.Presser, J.M.Romein, H.van Werveke. 12 vols. The Hague, 1949 - 1958. A very full handbook with helpful bibliographies in each volume.

H.de Buck, **Bibliografie der Nederlandse geschiedenis** Leiden, 1968. An selective and extensive bibliography.

# Selected list of places of historical interest

**Early History**
Hunebeds in Drente.
Provincial Museum in Assen (objects from hunebeds and peat-bogs).
Rijksmuseum of Antiquities in Leiden (objects before 1000!.
Bonnefantenmuseum in Maastricht (objects found in South Limburg).
Mounds ('terps') in the neighbourhood of Dokkum.

**Middle Ages**
Sint Servaas Church and Our Lady's Church in Maastricht (Roman). Both have exhibits of church treasures.
Cathedral in Utrecht (with separate tower) (early Gothic).
St.John's Cathedral in 's-Hertogenbosch (late Gothic).
St.Bavo Church in Haarlem (Gothic).
Castle Loevestein near Brakel (14th century castle, beautifully situated on the intersection of great rivers. Nice trip by boat from Gorkum).
Rijksmuseum Muiderslot in Muiden (well-preserved, medieval castle with 17th century furniture, with view on former Zuyder Zee).

Beautiful medieval town lay-out with many late-medieval buildings still well-preserved in the towns of Veere, Den Briel, Zierikzee and Elburg.
Archi-episcopal Museum in Utrecht (medieval religious art).

**Republic** (16th, 17th & 18th centuries)
*General*
Museum Prinsenhof in Delft (old convent, residence of William the Silent. Objects of Dutch history and the House of Orange-Nassau shown).
Historical Section of Rijksmuseum in Amsterdam (Netherlands from 1600, many paintings, ship models, etc. Modern display).
Netherlands Nautical Museum in Amsterdam (ship models, drawings, plans etc.).
Maritime Museum 'Prins Hendrik' in Rotterdam (ship models etc. from the 16th century).
Archeological and Naval Museum in Middelbuurt, North-East Polder, and Ketelhaven, East Flevoland (many remainders of ships and utensils found on the bottom of the Zuyder Zee during reclamation work. In Ketelhaven some very well-preserved ship skeletons are shown).
16th and 17th century city centres of Amsterdam (boat trips), Bolsward, Delft, Edam, Hoorn, Hindeloopen, Leiden, Oudewater.
17th century fortress-towns, still well-preserved: Naarden and Willemstad.
Netherlands Army Museum 'Generaal Hoefer' in Leiden (collection of arms, uniforms etc. from the 15th century onwards).

*History of Art*
Rijksmuseum in Amsterdam (great collection of paintings 14th - 19th century).
Mauritshuis in The Hague (exquisite collection of 17th century paintings).
Museum Boymans van Beuningen in Rotterdam (high quality paintings from the 16th century).
Frans Halsmuseum in Haarlem (example of charming city museum with good collection of Haarlem painters such as Hals).

*Buildings*

'Binnenhof' (Inner Court) in The Hague (oldest parts dating from the Middle Ages, used as governmental buildings since the 16th century, today for both Houses of Parliament).

'Palace' on the Dam in Amsterdam (built in the 17th century as the Town Hall).

Examples of some of the many interesting bourgeois mansions along Amsterdam canals (mostly built in the 18th century): Willet Holthuysen Museum and Theatrical Museum ('Toneelmuseum') in Amsterdam (interior decorations of doors, hall and staircase should also be seen).

'Het Huys ten Bosch' in The Hague (palace built in the 17th century by the Stadtholder, still a royal palace, one of the few examples of baroque palacebuilding in the Netherlands).

Protestant Churches during the 17th and 18th centuries: Lutheran cupola church in Amsterdam, Mare Church in Leiden and St. James' Church in The Hague (octagonal churches, because no altar was needed; churchbuilding for Protestants was exceptional because medieval churches were secularized, 'cleaned' and satisfied needs).

University building in Leiden (medieval convent with many later additions and interesting portraits, botanical gardens etc.).

*Curiosities*

'Librije' of the St.Walburgs' Church in Zutphen (old public library, 1561, with chained manuscripts and old books in church building).

Menkemaborg near Uithuizen (15th century noble residence with mostly 17th century interior decorations and furniture. Beautifully situated in flat Groninger land).

Heringastate in Marssum (example of noble estate of 18th century Frisian gentleman-farmers).

'Gevangenpoort' in The Hague (medieval prison-house still used in the 17th and 18th centuries. Most objects shown from this period).

'Heksenwaag' in Oudewater (17th century weighing-house which specialized in weighing old women and handing out certificates to disprove that they were witches, because of their 'human' weight).

Rijksmuseum 'Huis Lambert van Meerten' in Delft (curious 19th century neo-medieval house with great collection of Delft ware).
Rembrandthouse in Amsterdam (workshop of wealthy Rembrandt, with famous collection of Rembrandt prints and drawings).
Museum Amstelkring in Amsterdam (a 17th century Roman Catholic 'hidden' church).
Bibliotheca Thysiana in Leiden (collection of books in small library building built for that purpose by a private book-collector of the 17th century).
Zaans Molenmuseum in Koog aan de Zaan (models of and objects from windmills).
Teyler's Museum in Haarlem (building and collection of natural history, mechanics, geology, prints, paintings and books of a wealthy private gentleman-collector in the second half of the 18th century).
17th century polder of the Beemster, north of Amsterdam (old farmhouses, pretty little towns like De Rijp etc., particularly beautiful during flowering of fruit trees).
'Czar Peter Huisje' in Zaandam (small dwelling of 1637, in which the Russian emperor lived when learning shipbuilding and sail-making in 1697).

**Kingdom** (19th & 20th centuries)
*General*
Historical Section of the Rijksmuseum in Amsterdam (in new display, some attention is also paid to late modern history).
Postal Museum in The Hague (nice modern display).
Netherlands Railway Museum in Utrecht (in old railway station).
Rijksmuseum for the History of the Sciences in Leiden (very full collection in too cramped a place, many instruments used for research at for example Leiden University).

*History of Art*
Rijksmuseum in Amsterdam (19th century paintings, Hague School).
Museum Boymans van Beuningen in Rotterdam (19th and 20th century paintings).
Municipal Museum in The Hague (19th and 20th century

paintings and applied arts in interesting 20th century building of Berlage).
Rijksmuseum Kröller-Müller, Hoge Veluwe (beautifully situated in attractive 20th century building also designed by Berlage. Modern art from 1870).
Municipal (Stedelijk) Museum in Amsterdam (modern art from 1890).
Van Gogh Museum (opening 1973) in Amsterdam (has together with Kröller-Müller the majority of the Van Goghs).
Municipal van Abbe Museum in Eindhoven (20th century paintings).

*Buildings etc.*
Rijksmuseum and Central Station in Amsterdam (Neo-Gothic late 19th century style. Architect: Cuypers).
Stock Exchange in Amsterdam (early 20th century, pioneering architecture by Berlage).
Building of the Nederlandse Handel Maatschappij in Amsterdam (1920s modern building by De Bazel).
'De Bijenkorf' building in The Hague (1920s, modern building by Kramer).
Residential areas in Amsterdam South (1920s and 1930s).
Modern middle and working class areas in Amsterdam West and East (from 1920 onwards).
Town Halls in Enschede, Hilversum and The Hague (modern public buildings of the 1930s).
New city centre of Rotterdam (post-war).
Provincial Houses in Arnhem and The Hague (post-war).

*Curiosities*
'De Cruquius' in Heemstede (first steam-driven pumping-station built in 1849 and fully preserved).
Panorama Mesdag in The Hague (large panorama of the old fishermen's village of Scheveningen, since then absorbed by The Hague, painted in 1881 by famous painters).
Anne Frank Huis in Amsterdam (old house in city centre where Anne Frank, who wrote there her famous diary, had to be hidden during German occupation but was finally found by the Nazis).
War monuments (post-war) for example in Rotterdam of Zadkine, in Amsterdam the national monument on the Dam

(architect: Oud, sculptor: Rädecker) and the monument of
the general strike in February 1941 (sculptor: Andriessen)
in the Jonas Daniel Meijer Square, Amsterdam.
Zuyder Zee Dyke (Afsluitdijk) and new polders in the
Zuyder Zee.
Delta-works, south of Rotterdam in South Holland and
Zeeland islands (dykes, dams, bridges, sluices, etc.).
Great modern electrical pumping-station for Zuyder Zee
works near Lelystad (Flevo-centrale).

**General** (no special period, referring to two or three
periods)
*Ethnology and Folklore*
Open Air Museum in Arnhem (folklore, national costumes,
but in particular authentic houses, mills etc. Authentic
buildings rebuilt in beautiful surroundings).
Zuyder Zee Museum in Enkhuizen (many objects,
costumes, ship models etc. in modern display about the
fishing ports and areas around the Zuyder Zee).
Tropical Museum in Amsterdam (many objects, treasures,
folkloric handwork etc. from Dutch East Indies and
contemporary Indonesia).
Rijksmuseum of Ethnology in Leiden (many objects from
Dutch East Indies and contemporary Indonesia).

*Local and regional history*
Many cities have their own museums for the collection of
historical objects of the city or region. Some collections
very well displayed in historically and aesthetically
interesting buildings. A few only can be mentioned here:
The Amsterdam Historical Museum in Amsterdam.
The West-Frisian Museum in Hoorn.
The City Museum 'Catherina Gasthuis' in Gouda.
The Cloth Hall Museum in Leiden.
The Historical Museum of Rotterdam.
Many others could be mentioned such as the museums in
Amersfoort, Arnhem, Dordrecht, Enschede,
's-Hertogenbosch, Leeuwarden, Middelburg, Zwolle etc.